MADE IN THE MARGINS

NPLR

NEW PERSPECTIVES IN LATINA/O RELIGION

Miguel A. De La Torre
editor

OTHER BOOKS IN THIS SERIES

Miguel A. De La Torre, *Latina/o Social Ethics: Moving Beyond Eurocentric Moral Thinking*

MADE IN THE MARGINS

LATINA/O CONSTRUCTIONS OF U.S. RELIGIOUS HISTORY

HJAMIL A. MARTÍNEZ-VÁZQUEZ

BAYLOR UNIVERSITY PRESS

Waco, Texas 76798-7363

Cover Design by Nita Ybarra
Book Design by Diane Smith

Library of Congress Cataloging-in-Publication Data

Martínez-Vázquez, Hjamil A.
Made in the margins : Latina/o constructions of U.S. religious history / Hjamil A. Martínez-Vázquez.
p. cm. -- (New perspectives in Latina/o religion)
Includes bibliographical references (p. 175) and index.
ISBN 978-1-60258-199-9 (pbk. : alk. paper)
1. Hispanic Americans—Religion. 2. United States—Church history. 3. Christianity—Historiography. 4. Church history—Historiography. I. Title.
BR563.H57M365 2013
277.30089'68--dc23
2012028964

Printed in Canada on acid-free paper with a minimum of 30% pcw content.

Para Vanessa,
Inspiración continua,
Espacio de amor,
Y pasión verdadera.

CONTENTS

ACKNOWLEDGMENTS

Giving thanks is always a difficult task because of the danger of forgetting somebody. But it is important to acknowledge the work and *acompañamiento* of many friends and colleagues in the process of finishing this project since its initial stages during my dissertation. First, I have to thank the members of my dissertation committee, Kurt Hendel, José David Rodríguez, David Daniels, and William Fred Santiago. Their comments and solidarity toward my project, and its subversive content, make them deserving of much of the credit for its development and completion. Second, it is important to mention the companionship and help of two important people, Daisy L. Machado and Dale Irvin, who challenged me to take every argument here a little further. I am indebted to you!

Miguel De La Torre, thank you for taking a chance on this project and pushing me to see its possibilities. I am indebted to the CEHILA USA family, who always opened its doors to my interest on theories of histories; they have served as more than conversational partners, but as friends in the search for the decolonization of the dominant discourses. It is also important to acknowledge Mark Dennis, Scott Stirling, and Mathieu Weiss, whose companionship and support have been essential. Also, it is important to thank Corinne Adams and Sammie Bennett, my student assistants, who worked hard in the developmental stages of the project.

Finally, I want to thank some people whose support and inspiration have made this book possible. As always I am indebted to Arlene Sánchez-Walsh for her constant support and *acompañamiento*, and the space of trust she constantly provides, and to Sean McMillan, who always brought love and passion to our conversations and our dreams of a liberated knowledge. In addition, I am thankful to Kristina Smith, who always pushed me to be true to the spirit behind this project. To my brothers and sister, and their families: Omar Martínez-Vázquez, Edgardo Martínez-Vázquez, Isabel Martínez-Torres, Kalitza Baerga, Monica Rivera, Omar Ignacio, Gustavo Andrés, Alma Zoé, and Edgardo Luis, I carry you with me even in the distance. To my mother, Edda Vázquez-Beitía, and my father, Edgardo Martínez-Nazario, I hope this and all of my works make you proud. Finally, and as always, most importantly, I am grateful for the unconditional love and presence of my wife Vanessa González-López and our son Estéfano Martínez-González. You are the reason for my struggle for decolonization.

INTRODUCTION
WHY HISTORIOGRAPHY?

Historiography is the writing and study of history, yet in that writing theories are constructed, albeit unwittingly. The writing of history, I would argue, is the space in which historians build upon what has been written, thereby constructing theories that will become prominent ideologies of any given area of study. Historians theorize arguments in relation to studies, discursively formed, to agree or disagree with the specific field under scrutiny and its intellectual direction.

On the other hand, if one studies history only from a Foucauldian stance, to rupture totalities and dispute origins, one can become disillusioned; yet disillusion may be essential in order to interrogate differences and subjectivities in different ways, perhaps by crossing disciplines. The historian's subjectivity imagines and produces historiography, even when it is revisionist.

—Emma Pérez, *The Decolonial Imaginary*, 9, 32

While I was doing my graduate work, some of my professors told me that in order to get acquainted with U.S. religious history I needed to read Sydney E. Ahlstrom's *A Religious History of the American People* because it was the masterpiece in the field. After finishing the thousand-plus pages, I realized why it was such an important read. It was not because I found it to be a masterpiece, but because I found it to be an excellent representation of the traditional discourse that has left different groups and communities outside the historical consciousness. It was really hard to find stories within the discourse that focus on Latinas/os. Traditional U.S. religious historiography has created a canon in which the subaltern, *minoritized* communities do not acquire subjectivity.

The standard narrative in U.S. religious historiography is a colonial discourse in the sense that it silences voices and covers memories of whole groups. Even when revisions to the canon have opened the field to new voices and stories, these have not fully challenged the subject matter or the paradigms of interpretations. This canon positioned the subaltern at the margins of the text, as footnotes, and at the borderlands of society. The construction of this standard narrative followed the same path as traditional modern historical discourse since it became normative, and for a long time the content was seen as the past as it really happened. In this task, narrative became the form of discourse as well. In this standard (or master) narrative, the Protestant-Puritan tradition was the central aspect through which everything was interpreted. This discourse was given a universal character. Every other particularity, therefore, had to be explained through it in order to acquire any kind of validity. The modern project, embedded within this standard narrative, constructed an image of the subaltern that benefited the dominant groups. In the canon, the land the subaltern occupied is seen as empty and open for destruction, conquest, and colonization. Their memory is stolen and destroyed. It is said that nothing good can come from these people because of their characteristics of savagery and barbarity.[1] These images are constructed and imposed on the subaltern in order to maintain and increase the power of the dominant group, and the present racial/ethnic paradigm does not provide a critique of these misrepresentations and silences.

The history of the Southwest serves as one of the best examples for understanding these constructions and silences. Traditional U.S. religious historiography sees the Southwest and its history through the lens of progress and westward movement. Notions like the vacancy of the land, the conquest of the wilderness, and the superiority of the Euro-American race were supported by the ideology of Manifest Destiny embedded in the missionary activities of the first two centuries of Protestant growth in the United States. "To the extent that the Protestant heritage has been characteristic of the religious ethos of the United States in its first two centuries of

[1] See David J. Weber, *Myth and the History of the Hispanic Southwest* (Albuquerque: University of New Mexico Press, 1988).

growth, it might be said that Manifest Destiny expressed the ideological rationale of the Protestant empire."[2] Manifest Destiny established a culture of supremacy and racial domination.[3] It created a myth of a frontier, wilderness, and a virgin land. "America" is based on this myth, a sentiment of chosen people. Manifest Destiny and the myth it creates are still embedded in the writing of U.S. religious history. Although Frederick Jackson Turner's frontier thesis has been challenged and confronted, the sentiment behind it is still rooted in the beliefs of superiority and domination. The Southwest is not part of the imaginary as a space of encounter and exchange or subjectivity, but as an empty space available for conquest, progress, and missionary activity.

The canon of U.S. religious history, as a traditional historical discourse, can be characterized by its impetus for continuity. Every aspect that breaks that continuity, such as the presence of the Latina/o religious experiences, is thus left out. For example, since the histories of Latinas/os and Native Americans in the Southwest challenges the clean image of westward movement and progress, the canon has relegated these histories to a footnote, or ignores them altogether. But, as is the case with other colonial discourses, many counter-discourses continue to appear in order to challenge the character of normative historical knowledge In the case of traditional U.S. religious historiography, I argue that in targeting the production of knowledge, counter-discourses need to focus on the deconstruction of the canon, so that the larger picture it created is dismantled. I understand that some scholars would argue that this traditional canon has already been replaced with the additions of some voices and stories, and that attention to it is passé and unnecessary. A look at syllabi from courses in U.S. religious history reveals that while new topics have arisen and are being explored, the underlying matrix of the canon is still present, and even Latina/o voices

[2] Edwin Sylvest, "Hispanic American Protestantism in the United States," in *Fronteras: A History of the Latin American Church in the USA since 1513*, ed. Moises Sandoval (San Antonio, Tex.: Mexican American Cultural Center, 1983), 283.

[3] See Albert K. Weinberg, *Manifest Destiny: A Study of Nationalist Expansionism in American History* (Chicago: Quadrangle Books, 1935); Frederick Merk, *Manifest Destiny and Mission in American History: A Reinterpretation* (Westport, Conn.: Greenwood Press, 1963); and Thomas R. Hietala, *Manifest Design: Anxious Aggrandizement in Late Jacksonian America* (Ithaca, N.Y.: Cornell University Press, 1985).

are still absent or treated as outsiders to that history. Thus, there is still a need to construct counter-discourses that challenge the matrix. This book is about offering one perspective on the construction of one of these counter-discourses, these subaltern histories. Because Latina/o religious histories have been silenced by the canon, I argue that scholars of Latina/o religious history need to construct discourses that not only highlight the presence (*historicity*) of the experiences of these communities but also confront and deconstruct the coloniality within U.S. religious historiography.

Projects engaged in this confrontation must actually debunk the multicultural ideology that promotes the addition of new people into the normative discourse as objects (recipients) and not subjects of their own history. "The historian's political project, then, is to write a history that decolonizes otherness."[4] In order to achieve this deconstruction, scholars need to consider not only the stories but also the theories and methodologies used to construct historical narratives. In this regard, Charles H. Long argues,

> It is no longer possible for us to add the "invisible ones" as addenda to a European dominated historical method for such a procedure fails to take into account the relationships of the omitted ones to the Europeans throughout American religious history. Nor is it possible for us, simply in imitation of the historical method we are criticizing, to begin the project of writing history in which the ideological values of blacks and Amerindians dominate. This procedure has no merit for it could not make sense of that problem of invisibility which allowed us to raise the issue of our discussion. The issue raised here is a subtle one and questions must be asked concerning the very nature of historical method.[5]

Thus, it is important to dis-cover the silences that have been perpetuated by the standard narrative, but in order to give these silent voices the opportunity to speak about their own situation and in their own terms, we need new theories and methodologies that do not serve the colonial agenda. I argue that from a postcolonizing perspective it is possible construct subversive discourses that both

[4] Emma Pérez, *The Decolonial Imaginary: Writing Chicanas into History* (Bloomington: Indiana University Press, 1999), 6.

[5] Charles H. Long, "A New Look at American Religion," in *The Writing of American Religious History*, ed. Martin E. Marty (Munich: K.G. Saur, 1992), 87.

confront the canon of U.S. religious historiography and dis-cover the voices of the subaltern as subjects of history. But, for historians of the Latina/o religious experiences, as well as other subaltern communities, it is important to start thinking about our own theories and methodologies in order to reproduce the colonial process of representation.

THEORY AND SUBALTERNITY IN LATINA/O RELIGIOUS HISTORY

I understand that it is not common for historians to think about theory. Many historians, particularly U.S. religious historians, do not see theory and method as essential parts of their projects. They focus too much on the development of narratives and forget the importance of what lies behind those narratives and their purpose. However, postmodern historians have understood the limits of history as a discipline and for that matter argue for the need to bring theory back into the discussion of history. Theory, in this sense, should be understood as a paradigm of knowledge, a model, and not as a hypothesis. Theory allows the questioning of the rules and practices being used in academic institutionalized history and its exclusive character in the representation of knowledge about the past. These questionings engage history in its content and form. In a postcolonizing agenda for Latina/o religious historians, theory, thus, is essential, as it not only allows us to question the ideologies behind the canon of U.S. religious history, but also to analyze our own ideologies and lenses of interpretation in order to produce discourses that are specific and do not argue for any kind of universality.

This need for theory also implies the need to go beyond the traditional understandings of history and look into other disciplines that could help in our process of decolonizing the traditional narratives. "It means traversing new territories and disciplines, mapping fresh terrains such as cultural studies, women's studies, ethnic studies, and of course, Chicana/o studies."[6] I make this call to step beyond the traditional parameters of history in order to construct transdisciplinary methodologies that explore the subaltern's consciousness, not simply actions. Simply exploring actions only serves to narrativize the past through a process of emplotment as if it were actually a story, but exploring the consciousness of the subaltern opens the

[6] Pérez, *Decolonial Imaginary*, xiii.

door for a look at the past beyond a linear narrative. Breaking that false linearity within the traditional discourses allows us to notice the discontinuities of these. Our projects need to be engaged in in-depth analysis of these discontinuities because it is within these spaces that the subaltern voice resides. Only through a constant look at the way we actually construct our discourses will we be able to make sure that our projects are engaged within these processes.

For Latina/o religious historians the process begins with the recognition that Latina/o communities, as the subaltern, enact subversion against those systems of power through their religious activities. Once we are able to see these multiple and diverse experiences as moments of transgression of the subaltern, we are able to have the basis for the development of subaltern histories that challenge traditional ways of doing history. Historian Edwin David Aponte argues that Latina/o Protestantism serves as an alternative cultural and social space, which he refers to as subaltern counterpublics.[7] While he focuses on Latina/o Protestantism, I would submit that Latina/o religious experiences as a whole (including Latina/o Catholicism, Latina/o Muslim experiences, Latina/o Afro-Caribbean religious experiences, among others) fit this particular paradigm. Aponte finds that, "Latina/o Protestantism meets the definition of a subaltern counterpublic on the margins of dominant groups with power in a society. In its many manifestations Latina/o Protestantism as counterpublic recognizes and resists the status quo hegemony with its efforts of social, economic, and cultural dominance and colonization."[8] In other words, Latina/o religious experiences serve as counter-discourses. It is the task of the historian also to recognize these as spaces of resistance and subjectivity and translate that into the production of representations of the subaltern as subject.

The recognition of the subalternity of Latinas/os, then, leads to development of new theories and methodologies that focus on these experiences as relevant and transformative. This approach is something we could learn from both the South Asian Subaltern Studies Group and the Latin American Subaltern Studies Group. Aponte argues that, "Both groups call for a new type of historiography that

[7] Edwin David Aponte, "Views from the Margins: Constructing a History of Latina/o Protestantism," in *Hispanic Christian Thought at the Dawn of the 21st Century: Apuntes in Honor of Justo L. González*, ed. Alvin Padilla, Roberto Goizueta, and Eldin Villafañe (Nashville: Abingdon, 2005), 85–97.

[8] Aponte, "Views from the Margins," 91.

questions assumptions, both casual and ideological, which show preference for the dominant views. In this type of analysis subaltern counterpublics are recognized as distinct from dominant discourses and producing social effects that are internally recognizable, even while invisible to larger publics."[9] Therefore, these subaltern experiences are not to be interpreted through the same lenses the dominant discourses use to construct their modern narratives. The discursive spaces from which Latina/o religious historians construct their discourses have to be different from those within traditional historiography, and they have to be grounded upon the same subversive ideology embedded within subaltern experiences. In this book I offer suggestions regarding new theoretical and methodological approaches that allow the historian to reach these discursive spaces of transgression.

SOCIAL LOCATION AND AGENDA OF THE BOOK

I have always sustained that every discourse needs to be not only self-critical but also self-referential in order not to give the illusion that it is universal or objective. This work is no exception. I was born and raised in Puerto Rico, one of the oldest colonies in the world. By birth I had imposed on me the citizenship of the United States since Puerto Rico is a colonial territory of the United States. While I have been residing and working in the United States for almost a decade now, I still see myself as a Puerto Rican, even when the system *classifies* me as a Latino. Because of my background, I know the condition of coloniality and oppression from a perspective different than that from which Latinas/os, who were born and raised within the United States, have experienced it. It is from that perspective of a subaltern that I read narratives, formulate ideas, and deconstruct ideologies. I approach academic work as a political endeavor in which I, through a discursive practice, have the responsibility to enact change. I recognize the difference between my location within the academic setting and the actual work that members of the community perform in order to enact social change, but still I see them as complementary processes. In this sense, as was the case for historian Emma Pérez, "My interest remains social change, but my focus is to probe change as it is formed discursively, in the past, by the present."[10]

[9] Aponte, "Views from the Margins," 91.
[10] Pérez, *Decolonial Imaginary*, 32.

As a colonized being, I approach history from its underside. I look at traditional historical narratives for what they hide, not necessarily for what they actually say. That is how I read Ahlstrom's work and it is from that same point of view that I construct a project that focuses on what has been hidden. I do not argue that my approach is the only approach, but that it is one of the approaches available, and thus it is important to highlight not only what I see myself doing but also what I do not see myself doing.

Now, I believe Latina/o religious historiography is at a crossroads. Because of the emergence and growth of social scientific approaches to the study of Latina/o religious experiences, historians are left wondering if historical approaches are still useful within this new academic reality. Here, I suggest that these new approaches only serve to reinforce the work of the historian, especially if she/he is engaged in postcolonizing criticism. Of course, my project is not the first to call for a rethinking of the way scholars approach the study of Latina/o religions, but it is one of the first to focus solely on the discipline of history.[11] Although my enterprise, which is dedicated to the construction of possible methodological and theoretical approaches, can be placed within the discipline of philosophy of history, I am writing it from the perspective of a historian. I use different works and theories in developing my project, so this enterprise should be understood as an eclectic one. I will employ these theories critically, as no one theory can be seen as the sole foundation of my work.[12] This eclectic endeavor creates a theoretical scaffold for the study and writing of history.

My project does not entail the construction of any specific historical narrative, as I am focusing on the actual process. In light of this I can only talk about the possibilities of the approaches I introduce, not about their end result. Dipesh Chakrabarty states that "The project of provincializing 'Europe' refers to a history that does not yet exist; I can therefore speak of it only in a programmatic

[11] Miguel A. De La Torre and Gastón Espinosa, eds., *Rethinking Latino(a) Religion and Identity* (Cleveland, Ohio: Pilgrim Press, 2006); and Luis D. León, *La Llorona's Children: Religion, Life, and Death in the U.S.-Mexican Borderlands* (Berkeley: University of California Press, 2004).

[12] The reader will see the presence of postmodern criticism, postcolonizing criticism, border criticism, Chicana feminist criticism, and others within this endeavor.

manner."[13] This is exactly how I see my project of postcolonizing Latina/o religious history.

STRUCTURE OF THE BOOK

This book is divided into three parts. The first part deals with an analysis of U.S. religious historiography. In the first chapter, by examining the construction of a canon, I provide evidence that this field was constructed on the basis of a modernist perspective and that it left voices out of the normative discourse, thus developing into a colonial discourse. Then, I briefly look at different methodological approaches that signal the possible transformation of the field. In chapter 2, based on those new approaches, I explore how particular themes and motifs, geography, religious pluralism, among others, continue to signal the marginalization of Latina/o voices. In order to understand the motivation of this marginalization, I uncover the presence of a black/white paradigm within U.S. religious historiography. Only through the deconstruction of this paradigm can one begin dismantling the canon.

In the second part of the book, I offer an examination of the present condition of the field of Latina/o religious history. I divide the field in two major areas, Catholic histories and Protestant histories, not because I believe they are completely different, but because their different interests make it easier to analyze them separately. Chapter 3 includes a historiographical look at the development of Latina/o Catholic histories while chapter 4 does the same for Latina/o Protestant histories. In both of these chapters, I focus my analysis on the different theoretical and methodological approaches scholars have used to construct their projects. At the end of chapter 4, I then move to compare and contrast the development of these two areas in order to assess the present condition of the field of Latina/o religious history and the major methodological approaches being used.

The third part of the book is dedicated to the construction of methodological approaches Latina/o religious historians can use in the process of constructing Latina/o religious historical discourses as subaltern histories. In chapter 5, I develop the theoretical presuppositions for my project by examining the way subaltern histories

[13] Dipesh Chakrabarty, *Provincializing Europe: Postcolonial Thought and Historical Difference* (Princeton, N.J.: Princeton University Press, 2000), 42.

are constructed. Postcolonizing criticism serves as the foundation of that project. Based on this theoretical approach, I then move to consider two possible methodological approaches that would help in the construction of Latina/o religious histories as subaltern histories. Because Latina/o religious experiences are formed by daily activities within and outside religious institutions, I discuss the lived religion approach in chapter 6. Then, in the last chapter, I analyze feminist history as the second possible approach. In both of these chapters, I not only explore the way these approaches have been used, but mostly I offer a description of the way these should be used from a postcolonizing perspective in order to confront traditional U.S. religious historiography as a colonial discourse, and to dis-cover Latina/o religious histories as subversive discourses.

PART I

A LOOK AT U.S. RELIGIOUS HISTORIOGRAPHY

In this first part I examine and confront U.S. religious historiography. I examine the connection between the dominant discourse in the field and the modern/colonial system. Historians constructed U.S. religious historiography on the basis of a tradition that left many groups without a historical voice. For a long time the recognized canon operated without these voices. Without a doubt the field has evolved away from that tradition, but even some of the new approaches still leave out many voices. Because of this, it is important to confront both the canon and the new perspectives.

This part is divided into two chapters. The first deals with the construction of a canon in the field of U.S. religious historiography. In this section, I use Jerald C. Brauer's organizational framework of the development of the canon, although I go beyond it in the interpretation of more recent works.[1] This canon is based on a Protestant-Puritan tradition, and its development took over a century. From Robert Baird to Sydney E. Ahlstrom to Mark A. Noll, this canon faced changes and revisions, but the Protestant-Puritan tradition was still the dominant perspective within the canon. At the end of the chapter, I examine some of the methodological developments that have tried to introduce new options to the canon.

In the second chapter, I take a closer look at the themes and motifs U.S. religious historians introduced in the 1990s, through the engagement in micro-narratives. The problem with these projects is

[1] Jerald C. Brauer, "Changing Perspectives on Religion in America," in *Reinterpretation in American Church History*, ed. Jerald Brauer (Chicago: University of Chicago Press, 1968), 1–28.

that many voices are still left out of the discourse, and for the most part the voices that have been included are not part of the subject matter. In many ways, these voices are still seen as marginal to the field. In the second part of the chapter, I argue that traditional U.S. religious historiography has built and has been built upon a black/white paradigm. This paradigm is one of the major sources of sustainability for the canon, since it controls the voices and stories that are to be included in the dominant discourse.

While I understand that the analysis of these works and this tradition may appear to be dated, I argue that these actually need to be re-examined because they have served as the foundation of the dominant canon. At the same time it is important to acknowledge that I recognize the importance and significance of these works in the development of the field and in no way should my analysis be taken as disregarding their value, but rather as an exercise to continue to move the field forward.

1 THE CANON OF U.S. RELIGIOUS HISTORY

During the nineteenth century, historians in the United States started to collect information in order to construct a synthesis of the history of religion in the United States. Robert Baird, with his *Religion in America*, was the first person to write a synthesis of religion in the United States.[1] This work concentrated on the Puritan aspects of Christianity and divided the church population into Evangelicals and non-Evangelicals. The latter group, including the Roman Catholic Church, was only discussed in one section of the book. One of the purposes of the author was to argue that Christianity in the United States constituted the new Reformation. As Sydney E. Ahlstrom recognized, "This was not simply the first important panoramic history of American religion: it was a manifesto for worldwide reformation of Christianity that took American Protestant voluntaryism [*sic*] as its model."[2] Baird focused on this model because he saw it as "the consequence of the separation of church and state, which threw all religious groups onto their own resources of persuasion and self-support."[3] Regardless of the model he used,

[1] Robert Baird, *Religion in America; or An Account of the Origin, Relation to the State, and Present Conditions of the Evangelical Churches in the United States with Notices of the Unevangelical Denominations* (New York: Harper & Brothers, 1856). First published in Scotland in 1843.

[2] Sydney E. Ahlstrom, *A Religious History of the American People* (New Haven, Conn.: Yale University Press, 1972), 8.

[3] Jerald C. Brauer, "Changing Perspectives on Religion in America," in *Reinterpretation in American Church History*, ed. Jerald Brauer (Chicago: University of Chicago Press, 1968), 3.

Baird provided religious historians a perspective from which to view the history of religion in the United States, a perspective that lasted until the 1920s.[4] Thus, Robert Baird's *Religion in America* became the first piece of the puzzle in the construction of the canon of U.S. religious historiography.

Other scholars continued to build upon Baird's pioneering work. In 1887 Daniel Dorchester included the importance of the Catholic presence and was more critical of Protestantism in his work, *Christianity in the United States*.[5] However, as Ahlstrom acknowledges, "Baird's heavy evangelical and outspokenly nativist bias remains."[6] Leonard W. Bacon maintained the emphasis on the construction of a synthesis of religion in the United States, particularly of Protestantism, with his *A History of American Christianity*.[7] This time period is important because of the formation of the American Society of Church History in 1888 through the leadership of Philip Schaff. Bacon's work is part of the first project of the society, an entire series on religion in the United States edited by Schaff, who followed much of Baird's perspective.

Jerald Brauer argues that "it was not until the 1920s that a major shift in perspective developed and provided the second way of looking at the development of Christianity in America."[8] He mentioned the work of Henry Rowe as the initial work in the changing face of U.S. religious history. However, it was not until 1930 that William Warren Sweet's *The Story of Religions in America* opened a new episode in the construction of the canon of U.S. religious historiography.[9] Sweet became the leading religious historian in the United States. By focusing on the frontier thesis proposed by Frederick Jackson Turner, he located U.S. religious history outside the European setting. He suggested that Protestantism in the United States

[4] Brauer, "Changing Perspectives," 3.

[5] Daniel Dorchester, *Christianity in the United States from the First Settlement Down to the Present Time* (New York: Phillips & Hunt, 1888).

[6] Ahlstrom, *Religious History*, 9.

[7] Leonard W. Bacon, *A History of American Christianity* (New York: Christian Literature, 1897).

[8] Brauer, "Changing Perspectives," 4–5.

[9] Henry Rowe, *The History of Religion in the United States* (New York: Macmillan, 1924); and William Warren Sweet, *The Story of Religions in America* (New York: Harper & Brothers, 1930). It is important to acknowledge that later versions of Sweet's book used the singular form "religion" in the title.

was different than Protestantism in Europe, and the conditions of the frontier experience explain that difference. He states:

> The greatest accomplishment of America is the conquest of the continent, the greatest achievement of the American churches has been the extension of their work westward across the vast stretches of the continent, keeping abreast with the restless and ever moving population. The first task of the American churches after the Revolution was to follow this westward-moving population over the Alleghenies, thence across the Ohio and Mississippi basins, on over the plains and the western mountains to the Pacific. Throughout this whole period the churches were in continuous contact with frontier conditions and frontier needs, and no single fact is more significant in its influence upon American religion.[10]

In a later work Sweet continued to promote the importance of the frontier as the main force in religious development in the United States, closely tied with religious freedom and immigration.[11] He stepped away from Baird in the sense that he saw the frontier and not voluntarism as the key to explain U.S religious history, although much of the content of their narratives remained the same. Through this work the interpretation of religion in the United States shifted regions, from New England Puritanism to the Puritanism of the frontier, the westward movement. So in this sense, Sweet's new interpretation gave way to other histories that included a look at spaces outside the dominant northeastern setting.[12]

[10] Sweet, *Story of Religions in America*, 3.

[11] See William Warren Sweet, *The American Churches: An Interpretation* (New York: Abingdon-Cokesbury, 1947).

[12] The problem resides in the fact that the inclusion of the West in the religious history of the United States was based on Turner's frontier thesis. Frederick Jackson Turner proposed his thesis in a paper entitled, "The Significance of the Frontier in American History," which was first presented on July 12, 1893, at the American Historical Association meeting in Chicago, and later as an address to the State Historical Society of Wisconsin on December 14, 1893. It was printed in the *Annual Report of the American Historical Association for the Year 1893* and was later reprinted by Irvington Publishers as part of *The Irvington Reprint Series*, History Reprint H-214. I will not debate the validity of the frontier thesis since my argument speaks for itself against it, but it is important to acknowledge that this thesis has defined up until the present how the colonization of the Southwest has been interpreted: as a missionary activity in a vacant land. The frontier is seen as a

H. Richard Niebuhr is another key figure who, during the first decades of the twentieth century, offered new perspectives on the religious situation in the United States. In his work *The Kingdom of God in America*, a book that follows his notable *The Social Sources of Denominationalism*, Niebuhr writes a history of U.S. religion based on theological paradigms, especially that of the "kingdom of God."[13] As was the case with Sweet, one of Niebuhr's main purposes was to offer a perspective of the religious situation in the United States that reflected originality. The concept "kingdom of God" served this principle, as he makes clear when he states:

> The Kingdom of God in America, so regarded, is the American kingdom of God: it is not the individualization of a universal idea, the universalization of the particular. It represents not so much the impact of the gospel upon the New World as the use and adaptation of the gospel by the new society for its own purposes.[14]

Without a doubt this conception and understanding locates the condition of religion in the United States in a universal sphere, unique in its own terms. So the United States takes over the control of the "kingdom" and becomes the universal example of that "kingdom." Niebuhr explains this universalization by establishing the close relationship between Christianity and culture in the U.S. setting. This effort, as well as his argument that more attention should be given to religion as movements and not as institutions in order to understand the religious phenomenon in the United States, assisted in the development of a canon in U.S. religious history through the inclusion of

---

meeting place between savagery and civilization. This erases the historical voice of the native people who did, in fact, occupy much of these lands. See George Rogers Taylor, ed., *The Turner Thesis: Concerning the Role of Frontier in American History* (Lexington, Mass.: D. C. Heath, 1956); Ray Allen Billington, *The Far Western Frontier: 1830–1860* (New York: Harper & Row, 1956); and Ray Allen Billington, *Land of Savagery, Land of Promise: The European Image of the American Frontier in the Nineteenth Century* (Norman: University of Oklahoma Press, 1981).

[13] H. Richard Niebuhr, *The Kingdom of God in America* (New York: Willett, Clark, 1937; Hanover, N.H.: Wesleyan University Press, 1988). Citations refer to the 1988 edition. H. Richard Niebuhr, *The Social Sources of Denominationalism* (Cleveland: World Publishing, 1929). *The Social Sources of Denominationalism* is an essential resource to understand where the study of denominations and pluralism came from.

[14] Niebuhr, *Kingdom of God*, 9.

a socio-theological perspective. Without a doubt, this perspective brought new arguments to the table, but most of the issues and topics under discussion were still strongly related to Puritanism.[15]

Sidney E. Mead's *The Lively Experiment: The Shaping of Christianity in America*, a collection of essays, brought forth another way of interpreting the situation of religion in the United States: denominationalism.[16] Mead did not fully step away from the argument of the uniqueness of Christianity in the United States, but he intended to prove that this originality did not come out of a particular source, like the "methodistic-frontier" interpretation proposed by Sweet, but from the interaction of different forces. The interplay between the denominations paved the path to what he calls "Americanism." "Mead did not eschew the sociohistorical approach of his predecessors, but he brought in a totally new dimension through his interest in the history of ideas."[17] This historian took on the task of questioning and revising the previous ways of doing U.S. religious history in order to provide historians with better tools to write a better history.

Several historians answered some of Mead's challenges and continued to build a synthesis of religion in the United States. The content of their work included more material, but the main thread that connected their narrative continued to be the Puritan/New England story and its characters. Winthrop S. Hudson was one of the historians who followed Mead's argument. He agreed with Mead about the importance of denominationalism in the understanding of Christianity in the United States, especially Protestantism, and the lack of one particular root for that history. Hudson makes this clear in the first paragraph of his *American Protestantism*:

> At first sight, American Protestantism appears so varied and multiform as to preclude any attempt to deal with it as a single historical entity. Institutionally, American Protestantism is not one but many. It has no central organization. It has no officially adopted

[15] The same happened with some other works produced in the following decades, which built their arguments based on previous works. See Jerald C. Brauer, *Protestantism in America: A Narrative History* (Philadelphia: Westminster, 1953); and Clifton E. Olmstead, *History of Religion in the United States* (Englewood Cliffs, N.J.: Prentice Hall, 1960).

[16] Sidney E. Mead, *The Lively Experiment: The Shaping of Christianity in America* (New York: Harper & Row, 1963).

[17] Brauer, "Changing Perspectives," 11.

> creed. It is bound together by no universally accepted liturgical forms. The structures of discipline and government are diverse. There is no great leader in its past around whom its loyalties may cluster, nor any golden age to which it can look with nostalgia as a norm. Instead of a single history, American Protestantism seems to have only a series of histories—the histories of individual denominations.[18]

Although in this work he focused on Protestantism, Hudson sketched out a little bit of what he hoped to do later on, a more plural and diverse narrative. He did exactly that, four years later, when he published his masterpiece *Religion in America*.[19] He establishes from the outset that he did not intend "to chronicle the life of individual religious groups" but that his major purpose was "to depict the religious life of the American people in interaction with other dimensions of their experience, and to depict the unity American religious life exhibits as well as its particularities."[20] Hudson accomplished a more pluralistic narrative with the inclusion of other religious groups and ideas outside Protestantism since he thought of religious pluralism as the present situation in the United States. A shortcoming in this work is that non-Protestant groups take on the status of outsiders within the narrative. Hudson's narrative still positioned Puritan-Protestantism at the center and other groups at the periphery. For this reason, Hudson did not use much of the material he introduced about religious pluralism as a way of challenging the basic understanding of Protestantism itself.

Edwin S. Gaustad followed the same path as Hudson in his work *A Religious History of America*.[21] Gaustad focused on the issue of religion and proposed that religion serves as one of the best paradigms to understand the history of the United States. In a sense, he wanted to promote the issue of religion for the broader field of historical studies and prove that it was and still is a paradigm that

[18] Winthrop S. Hudson, *American Protestantism* (Chicago: University of Chicago Press, 1961), 1.

[19] Winthrop S. Hudson, *Religion in America* (New York: Charles Scribner's Sons, 1965). Later versions of the book included the subtitle "An Historical Account of the Development of American Religious Life."

[20] Hudson, *Religion in America*, viii.

[21] Edwin S. Gaustad, *A Religious History of America* (New York: Harper & Row, 1966).

can explain colonization, expansion, and the rise of an empire. As in Hudson's *Religion in America*, and in most of the earlier works, the method employed in the writing is narrative, but significantly, its flow is not interrupted by mentioning non-Protestant groups since they are kept outside the main course of the narrative. This, again, prevented a thorough critique of the Protestant aspects of the religious experience in the United States. The same happened with the two-volume work *American Christianity: An Historical Interpretation with Representative Documents*, which included a large quantity of material in a cohesive arrangement, but the generalizations and presuppositions within the text were the same as in previous works, namely, Puritan-Protestantism as the center.[22]

By this period (the 1960s) the canon in U.S. religious historiography was opening up to religious pluralism, as the works by Hudson and Gaustad prove, although in a nonintegrative way. All this process had its climax in the writing of *A Religious History of the American People* by Sydney E. Ahlstrom. This work became the grand narrative of U.S. religious history, the conclusion of a tradition. Ahlstrom takes the narrative method to a new stage in the discipline because, while previous works were important, this piece acquired a normative status. Ahlstrom put "everything" together in one story. In other words, *A Religious History of the United States* became the canon of U.S. religious historiography. As Jerald C. Brauer pointed out right after this book came out, "This became the classical way of interpreting and writing the religious history of the United States. Sydney E. Ahlstrom has produced the definitive history in this tradition."[23] Brauer finds that the scholars in this tradition, those I have mentioned above, followed two assumptions: 1) It was possible, even with the diversity in denominations, "to sketch out a unified picture of the development of religion in America and to place it, in varying degrees, in dialogue with a complex social context"; and 2) There was a particularity in the structure of the religious experience in the United States, "particularly European yet Uniquely American—a Protestant reality," which shaped and formed the history.[24]

[22] H. Shelton Smith, Robert T. Handy, and Lefferts A. Loetscher, *American Christianity: An Historical Interpretation with Representative Documents*. 2 vols. (New York: Charles Scribner's Sons, 1960–1963).

[23] Jerald C. Brauer, "Review of *A Religious History of the American People*, by Sydney E. Ahlstrom," *Church History* 42, no. 3 (1973): 406.

[24] Brauer, "Review," 406.

Sydney E. Ahlstrom completed the work of the historians in the tradition that he followed, from Baird to Gaustad. Though this tradition, as I have pointed out, experienced changes through time, it was complete with this piece. Ahlstrom reinterpreted most of the main material uncovered by earlier historians, giving a new meaning to the understanding of religion in the United States by trying to focus on religion, and not merely Protestantism. In this regard, Henry Warner Bowden argues, "Ahlstrom's publication is a landmark in modern historiography, because it adequately summarizes the best work of colleagues to date and will provide the standard correlation of such material until decades of new spade-work require another one."[25] He set out to write a revisionist history of religion in the United States, a new perspective, but, as Brauer points out, that was not accomplished. Brauer affirms, "Though there are a number of important differences between Ahlstrom and his predecessors, such as his comprehensiveness, the far greater weight he gives to intellectual history, his attention to groups previously ignored or given inadequate treatment, the suppression of a particular chauvinism which marked Baird or Sweet, the fact remains that this is not a new interpretative perspective on religion in America which essentially rearranges our basic understanding of that history."[26] The amplitude of this work provided the space for several movements and religious experiences to be analyzed, but "the classic 'Protestant-Puritan' tradition remains the interpretative center of his history."[27] Although arguing for a renovation and a new paradigm in U.S. religious historiography, Ahlstrom continued to focus on the "Protestant-Puritan" tradition in order to construct his narrative to the point that it could be considered "one of the very best synthetic constructs of the development and role of that tradition in America."[28] I go a little further and argue that this became the canon of religious history in the United States and that the classical historiographical interpretation culminated in this work.

[25] Henry Warner Bowden, "Landmarks in American Religious Historiography: A Review Essay," in *The Writing of American Religious History*, ed. Martin E. Marty (Munich: K.G. Saur, 1992), 128.

[26] Brauer, "Review," 406.

[27] Brauer, "Review," 407.

[28] Brauer, "Review," 407.

Sydney E. Ahlstrom built this narrative on the tradition that preceded him, but the inclusion of religious pluralism is what makes his work so important. As David Daniels argues, "the Ahlstrom narrative serves as an apologia for religious pluralism."[29] He saw the United States of his time as a post-Puritan era and thought of its history as a process in which different religious groups developed and helped in the developing of the nation. Of course, he was not the first to include religious pluralism; Hudson and Gaustad had already done so. However, the massive space he dedicated to it provided a better opportunity of proving its importance. The problem with Ahlstrom's work is that he did not see this religious pluralism as a new way of interpretation, and the historiographical paradigm he set out to revise was kept unchanged. I therefore agree with Henry Bowden's statement that this work did not provide any detailed revision, but that it merely added new material to the already established tradition.[30]

A Religious History of the American People thus served the purpose of summarizing material and introducing new material, but it did not change the basic point of view of interpretation, which remained the "Protestant-Puritan" tradition. It opened the door for new research, but it did not contribute to the changing of lenses through which the historian interprets, reconstructs, and represents the past. Even though Ahlstrom indicated that the black experience is crucial in the study of religion in the United States and that it is the "basic paradigm for a renovation of American church history,"[31] he did not build new historiographical scaffolds based on this experience. The inclusion of religious pluralism and the black experience are not integral parts of the central theme of the book. They are included only as they are related to the Puritan tradition. Even in the last section of the book, the relationship to Puritanism is made by referring to a post-Puritan era. This gives Puritanism the central role in the interpretation of U.S. religious history, and everything else has to be referenced to its relationship to Puritanism. This is also what happened to religious pluralism and the black experience.

[29] David Daniels, "Teaching the History of U.S. Christianity in a Global Perspective," *Theological Education* 29, no. 2 (1993): 94.

[30] Bowden, "Landmarks," 133.

[31] Ahlstrom, *A Religious History*, 12.

Other scholars have assembled new narratives since, not of the magnitude of Ahlstrom's, but with somewhat the same basic commitment. This does not mean that they strictly followed the Ahlstrom tradition, but they built upon that tradition in order to promote shifts in the basic understanding of religious history in the United States. These works opened up the field to new dimensions and perspectives, but the dominance of the Protestant-Puritan tradition prevailed at the core of the narratives. Certainly, the black experience was included in most of the latter work. Historians dedicated chapters to the exploration of the material on this issue, but it was still seen as a separate aspect of the story, not as part of the larger narrative. Robert T. Handy, Martin E. Marty, and Mark A. Noll are three of these historians.[32] Handy's work on the history of Christianity in the United States and Canada broke a frontier in the discipline. He acknowledged the importance of Catholicism and with it the essential contact with the religious situation in Canada. Interestingly enough, Handy still saw voluntarism as the hermeneutical key to understand the religious experience on the continent, and, most importantly, he recognized the differences and similarities between the situations in Canada and the United States. It seems that this author saw these situations, with all their differences and particularity, as one.

Martin E. Marty continued the emphasis on pluralism. He used the concept of pilgrims to clarify the religious situation in the United States. For Marty, the constant movement of people helped to explain the religious history of the country. He challenged some of the earlier presuppositions about religious history by focusing on issues of dissent, exclusion, and religious pluralism. Near the end of *Pilgrims in Their Own Land* he proposed a more careful look at racial, ethnic, personal, and community movements, but he did not fully explore their interpretative possibilities. Although the center

[32] Robert T. Handy, *A History of the Churches in the United States and Canada* (New York: Oxford University Press, 1977); Martin E. Marty, *Pilgrims in Their Own Land: 500 Years of Religion in America* (Boston: Little Brown, 1984); and Mark A. Noll, *A History of Christianity in the United States and Canada* (Grand Rapids: Eerdmans, 1992). Other works in the area revised editions of previous works. See Edwin Scott Gaustad, *A Religious History of America*, new rev. ed. (San Francisco: Harper San Francisco, 1990); and Winthrop S. Hudson and John Corrigan, *Religion in America: An Historical Account of the Development of American Religious Life* (Upper Saddle River, N.J.: Prentice Hall, 1999).

of his interpretation is still related to the earlier tradition, Marty built an extensive new narrative that focused on pluralism and difference and which opened the field to the study of new dimensions, not only the Protestant-Puritan world.

Mark A. Noll, as Handy, also included Canada, and, as Marty, continued to explore and expand the material on and the dimensions of pluralism. He states his purpose clearly in the beginning of the book: "As a history, it is intended to provide certain basic information about some of the most important themes, events, leaders, and changes in the Christian churches that have populated the upper two-thirds of the North American continent over the last four centuries."[33] Noll opens the door to new topics as he argues,

> In particular, the fresh attention being paid to the experiences of women, nonwhites, and "ordinary" people who did not leave extensive written records has left its mark on the pages that follow. It may still not be entirely clear how to integrate such groups fully into the written story of Christianity in America, which until recently has been dominated by leaders of elite groups who did leave extensive published records.[34]

At the same time, Noll also argued that the Protestants of British background supplied the cohesive thread of North American religious history.[35] This clearly indicates that he did not locate himself outside the classical tradition and that even with the attention paid to the previously unrepresented communities, he, as Marty, could not escape the "Protestant-Puritan" ghost. In this sense, Noll's work is no different from others I have mentioned because he did not provide new interpretative scaffolds. He did, in fact, introduce new material through the already available lenses, those of the classical tradition. Without a doubt, through the inclusion of the experiences of the previously unrepresented communities, this author opens the field to new material, but that material is still considered to be peripheral to the basic theme and plot of the history, which is "the rise and decline of Protestant dominance in the United States."[36]

[33] Noll, *History of Christianity*, 1.
[34] Noll, *History of Christianity*, 1.
[35] Noll, *History of Christianity*, 2.
[36] Noll, *History of Christianity*, 4.

Although Marty and Noll revealed novel standpoints, they did not fully break away from the canon.

The canon, which had its initial document in Baird's work and its definitive study in Ahlstrom's work, has been characterized by its intimate relationship to the Protestant-Puritan world and the inclusion of other material from other religious groups and some other unrepresented groups. I go further to describe this canon as a closed standard narrative, which sees groups, experiences, and ideas outside the classical tradition as the Other. Religious pluralism has been addressed within the canon but has never become part of it, and as far as the black experience goes it has not been seen, as Ahlstrom proposed, as the basic paradigm of renovation of the discipline.

As I mentioned before, the black experience became an important research topic for many scholars and a large amount of material was uncovered and included in the standard narrative. In a sense, the inclusion of the black experience has been seen as the key aspect to complete the narrative, which does not mean that the black experience has taken a protagonistic role within it. Race has become an important issue but many times it has been treated as a "somewhat separate topic to be added to the already existing topics in the story of religion in America," and, as Roger D. Hatch further argues, this issue becomes relevant to monographs, additional chapters, or sections in established works.[37] Thus, race has not been an integrative part of the main topic and theme of the standard narrative. Historians who have followed the canon believe that the inclusion of new materials related to these issues is sufficient, but they have not revised the major arguments in light of these materials or in light of the issue of race. Hatch concludes:

> Thus the most important step in adequately integrating the issue of race into the story of Christianity in America comes at the very beginning, it comes in defining the subject matter. As long as the issue of race is not adequately integrated into an understanding of what the subject of a history is, it will not be integrated into

[37] Roger D. Hatch, "Integrating the Issue of Race into the History of Christianity in America: An Essay-Review of Sydney E. Ahlstrom, *A Religious History of the American People*, in Marty, *Writing of American Religious History*, 181; Martin E. Marty, *Righteous Empire: The Protestant Experience in America* (New York: Dial, 1970); and Robert T. Handy, *A Christian America: Protestant Hopes and Historical Realities* (Oxford: Oxford University Press, 1984).

> the story. As long as race is assumed to be something external to Christianity, the issue of race will not be adequately integrated into the story of Christianity in America.[38]

The canon, the standard narrative, has been closed to the issue of race and other issues as part of its subject matter because of its dependence on the modern project, which "assumed a universal truth with core and periphery relations, giving privilege to the rationality and sensibility that undergirded its cosmology as normative."[39] This traditional way of writing U.S. religious history follows the modernist impulse as it locates the Protestant-Puritan tradition at the center and other issues at the periphery and tends to universalize this tradition, leaving groups outside this experience without an actual participation in the historical project. So these groups, as subaltern, are left without a historical voice or consciousness. The standard narrative maintained the privileged position of U.S., white, male, Protestant America at the center through its use of power in writing, leaving hidden, or at the margin of the page as a footnote, the voices and stories of the subaltern. So, while some voices and stories were uncovered, the basic interpretative framework stayed the same. In its representation, the narrative constructs the past through the use of emplotment in which the events are seen in a progressive and continuous way from the European Reformation to an authentic U.S. Christianity to a religious plurality. Of course, the main catalyst, which explains this progressive character, is the Protestant-Puritan tradition that serves, as Noll acknowledges, as the thread of the narrative. This thread binds the interpretation and definition of all the material. It is in this sense that a connection can be made between this standard narrative (canon) and the idea of universal history or Foucault's *total* history, which I further discuss in the third part of this book. This standard narrative, then, becomes the dominant discourse, which creates an imaginary that becomes the norm and tends to be universalized. This imaginary is a colonial imaginary since it is sustained by the modern project.

On the other hand, it is also significant to acknowledge that Hayden White's argument about the use of narrative form can be used to analyze this canon. In these works as in other historical

[38] Hatch, "Integrating the Issue of Race," 205.

[39] Daniels, "Teaching the History," 95.

accounts, narrative has been used to establish the presence of a coherent argument without gaps or empty spaces.[40] Narrative as a form has provided U.S. religious historians a structure to construct one grand synthesis in which each event included is connected to every other. If an event, theme, or geographical space does not have a connection with the main argument of the narrative, it is left out or included as peripheral (footnote). Hence, the voices and stories that break the continuity are seen as secondary and nonessential. This provides the central thread in the narrative with a superior character and the people represented through it with a central role in society since they have a historical voice and consciousness. Through the use of these master narratives, power is enforced in order to omit and silence voices, just as in most colonial discourses. This canon is a colonial discourse because it relegates the subaltern to the borders and imposes a standard narrative (a master narrative) that has "focused disproportionately on male, northeastern, Anglo-Saxon, mainline Protestants and their beliefs, institutions, and power."[41] It has been used as the means by which voices have been silenced and memories hidden. Thus, traditional U.S. religious historiography works within the contours of the modern/colonial system. "The older versions have omitted key events, neglected important constituents, and failed to consider a diversity of points of view. They have, in short, given us a narrative that is truncated and short-sighted, dominated by a Protestant elite, and riddled with prejudice."[42]

NEW APPROACHES

In the past decades, there have been several new approaches to the writing of U.S. religious history. These approaches and perspectives are the result of historians following and building on issues mentioned, but not fully incorporated, previously by historians from Hudson to Ahlstrom and from Handy to Noll. They challenge the topics and the perspectives within the field by incorporating interdisciplinary approaches. Two important examples of works that have

[40] See Hayden White, *The Content of the Form: Narrative Discourse and Historical Representation* (Baltimore: Johns Hopkins University Press, 1987).

[41] Thomas A. Tweed, "Introduction: Narrating U.S. Religious History," in *Retelling U.S. Religious History*, ed. Thomas A. Tweed (Berkeley: University of California Press, 1997), 3.

[42] Steve McKinzie, "Saints and Revisionists: Refashioning the American Religious Narrative," *Cross Currents* 48, no. 1 (1998): 103.

challenged the canonical interpretations are Catherine L. Albanese's *America: Religions and Religion* and R. Laurence Moore's *Religious Outsiders and the Making of Americans,* which offer new perspectives on religious pluralism in the United States.[43] A close look at these books lies beyond the scope of my work, but it is important to point out their major arguments since their work is crucial because of their understanding of religious diversity and the introduction of new themes and geographical settings (outside New England).

Catherine Albanese follows a narrative approach in her writing but her narrative does not have the Protestant-Puritan tradition at its core since she argues that this tradition needs to be examined. She breaks away from this tradition by incorporating new material that proves the diversity in the U.S. religious arena, and her work has continued the process of opening spaces for new voices and showing directions to follow. Moore continues this project by challenging the dominance of Protestants in the writing of U.S. religious history. He has recognized the importance of Marty, Gaustad, and Ahlstrom in the process of uncovering voices and diversity, stating:

> Nonetheless, they and others have been able to look at the facts of religious diversity without trying to minimize them or explain them away. Consequently, they have prepared the way for the sympathetic treatment of subjects formerly regarded as merely outlandish. And they have called attention to huge areas of American religious experience, especially in the nineteenth century, that have received not nearly sufficient attention—black churches, the immigrant churches, and the uncountable number of independent churches.[44]

Moore goes beyond these scholars in order to prove that religious groups that have been left out of the canon, those he calls religious outsiders, "have been an indispensably dynamic force in American religious history."[45] David Daniels argues that "R. Lawrence Moore's concept of religious outsiders suggests a means to revise the narrative, offering a framework to discuss heterogeneity and to link plurality

[43] R. Laurence Moore, *Religious Outsiders and the Making of Americans* (New York: Oxford University Press, 1986); and Catherine L. Albanese, *America: Religions and Religion* (Belmont, Calif.: Wadsworth, 1992).

[44] Moore, *Religious Outsiders,* 20.

[45] Moore, *Religious Outsiders,* 21.

and commonality."[46] Moore confronts the divisions between mainstream and periphery, between mainline and nonmainline, since he argues that those outsiders are part of the portrait of what it means to be "American." By doing this, he has challenged the canon of U.S. religious historiography.

These two works are examples of the different lenses for interpretation scholars have proposed within U.S. religious historiography. Both of them found in religious pluralism the major paradigm that causes the shift in interpretation. These challenges have inspired further projects dealing with nonmainstream religious groups and movements and with the development of new ways of understanding religion in the United States. Robert A. Orsi's *The Madonna of 115th Street: Faith and Community in Italian Harlem, 1880–1950* and Peter W. Williams' *America's Religions: Traditions and Cultures* are two other examples of projects that have introduced new ways of understanding and studying religion with the incorporation of material on popular religion.[47] They promote the discussion and the incorporation of the issue of class within the religious historical discourse in the United States. Both projects propose a change in the way that religion should be understood and studied by introducing an interdisciplinary approach to it, in particular the use of ethnography. This kind of approach can be seen as part of the "new religious history."[48] This "new religious history" has been seen as an "interdisciplinary trend that began in the 1950s and was further stimulated after 1976 by the activities of the Religion and Society Network of the Social Science History Association."[49] In this sense, this trend was not developed within the U.S. religious historical field, but did indeed open this field to new perspectives. The "new religious history" is conceptualized in this way:

[46] Daniels, "Teaching the History," 98.

[47] Robert A. Orsi, *The Madonna of 115th Street: Faith and Community in Italian Harlem, 1880–1950* (New Haven, Conn.: Yale University Press, 2002); and Peter W. Williams, *America's Religions: Traditions and Cultures* (New York: Macmillan, 1990).

[48] See Philip R. Vandermeer and Robert P. Swierenga, eds., *Belief & Behavior: Essays in the New Religious History* (New Brunswick, N.J.: Rutgers University Press, 1991).

[49] Philip R. Vandermeer and Robert P. Swierenga, "Introduction: Progress and Prospects in the New Religious History," in Vandermeer and Swierenga, *Belief & Behavior*, 4.

> Whether emerging from traditional questions or new interests within religious history, or drawn by contact with historians seeking to explain behavioral patterns in their subfields of political, economic, or social history, these studies share a common approach. Their work is analytical rather than narrative; it employs theory and models; it often (though not always) evaluates quantitative data; and its subjects are recurrent not unique events, groups rather than individuals, and general patterns often examined through case studies.[50]

This kind of history has expanded the discussion within the larger historical field, but it was not until the last two decades that it has made its way into the core of the traditional U.S. religious historical field. This is not to say that no religious historian had worked within the scope of these new trends.

Some of the new perspectives focus on popular religion, feminism and other gender issues, immigration, and religious pluralism, among others. Presently, "lived religion" is one of those perspectives that has been brought forward, which I will fully examine in chapter 6. As Robert A. Orsi affirms:

> The study of lived religion explores how religion is shaped by and shapes the ways family life is organized, for instance: how the dead are buried, children disciplined, the past and future imagined, moral boundaries established and challenged, homes constructed, maintained, and destroyed, the gods and spirits worshiped and importuned, and so on. Religion is approached in its place within a more broadly conceived and described lifeworld, the domain of everyday existence, practical activity, and shared understandings, with all its crises, surprises, satisfactions, frustrations, joys, desires, hopes, fears, and limitations.[51]

This kind of approach could be compared to the history of everyday life. This serves as an example that religious history in fact has been opening itself to new methodological and interdisciplinary trends, which I will later refer to as a sociological turn in the field.[52]

[50] Vandermeer and Swierenga, "Introduction," 4.

[51] Orsi, *Madonna of 115th Street,* xiii–xiv.

[52] The work of Robert Wuthnow should be recognized since it proposes a restructuring in the interpretation of religion in the United States based on the

However, the discussion cannot be left here. While these new trends have made their way into the field of U.S. religious history and have helped the field expose some of the silences, other voices and stories are still covered and hidden, like the Latina/o religious experience. It is important, then, to take a look at the major themes and motifs in the scholarship.

---

relationship between politics and faith. See Robert Wuthnow, *The Restructuring of American Religion: Society and Faith since World War II* (Princeton, N.J.: Princeton University Press, 1988). Rhys Isaac, *The Transformation of Virginia, 1740–1790* (Chapel Hill: University of North Carolina Press, 1982), also needs to be acknowledged for the use of cultural anthropology in the historical understanding of a particular society.

2 NEW THEMES, OLD SILENCES

During the 1990s anthologies and collections of article-length essays replaced the larger volume-long works of history within U.S. religious historiography since the smaller works could focus more narrowly on specific regions, themes, particular historical figures, communities, religions, and/or periods of time. It is within these new narratives that one needs to look in order to dis-cover whether the change in approaches actually has generated a change in the themes and motifs of U.S. religious history. In these anthologies, scholars are proposing new directions and perspectives while, at the same time, some are promoting the continuation of the traditional historiography in a subtle way. In other words, while some scholars challenge the traditional model of writing the history of the U.S. religious experience, others take new approaches but still maintain the content of the canon.[1] In this chapter, I explore some of the themes within these anthologies in order to show that even with the development of new approaches, Latina/o religious

[1] It should be established that the shortcoming of these micro-narratives is that most of them do not make connections to a larger project, and the studies are seen as particular and not related to the experience of society. Micro-narratives, as does every historical project, participate in the process of silencing, but the explicit self-awareness of these silences and the establishment of points of continuity or discontinuity with other micro-narratives is crucial. In this sense, it is important to establish connections between these micro-narratives in order to construct a larger project. This project should not be a particular macro-narrative since macro-narratives are usually built upon the dichotomy center/periphery, which actually participates in the covering of voices. This should be done through the development of interrelated discourses.

experiences are left out. Even further, traditional U.S. religious historiography has constructed a black/white paradigm that controls the discourse, leaving the subaltern that does not fit this paradigm (e.g., Latinas/os) outside the official historical narratives.

NEW THEMES AND MOTIFS

I begin with an examination of *Retelling U.S. Religious History*, edited by Thomas A. Tweed, which shows that the grand narratives have left certain regions and communities out of the normative historical account.[2] Scholars in this book uncover the religious story of different regions of the United States. The "aim is not to reconstruct a single grand narrative, but to offer several situated stories and ask readers whether these illumine regions of the past that had remained obscured in the older surveys."[3] This work demonstrates the importance of considering geographical location as a locus of analysis. This shift not only highlights the history of other geographical spaces within U.S. religious history, but it also recuperates the voices of people in the borderlands both geographically and socially. Lauren F. Winner points to the importance of this approach to the recovery of marginalized voices as she states, "the scholars in *Retelling U.S. Religious History* rightly insist on showing that 'outsiders,' to alter the metaphor, are more than just raisins in the cake."[4] This is a way of breaking away from the normative discourse by establishing the presence of other legitimate stories previously absent from the standard narrative.

The authors in this anthology find that motifs (sexuality, contact and exchange, colonialism) and locations (Canadian borders, the southwestern territory, Pan-Pacific area) serve as important hermeneutical keys in order to bring new perspectives to the table. It is important for them to do this recovery, this "retelling," because the absence of a group in a discourse is more than the absence of a voice. In the introduction of the book, Tweed argues:

[2] Thomas A. Tweed, ed., *Retelling U.S. Religious History* (Berkeley: University of California Press, 1997).

[3] Thomas A. Tweed, "Introduction: Narrating U.S. Religious History," in Tweed, *Retelling*, 6.

[4] Lauren F. Winner, "Retold, Redirected, Rethunk: Form and Content in the Study of American Religion," *Books and Culture: A Christian Review* 4, no. 3 (1998): 21.

> The stories that fill history textbooks are important because they negotiate power and construct identity. They situate us in society and tell us who we are. Historical narratives often reflect, and shape, the social and economic order: individuals and groups excluded from narratives are excluded from more than stories. Those who do not find themselves or their experience represented in the most widely told stories engage in struggles—private and public, quiet and noisy—to make sense of themselves and locate their place among others in the wider society. Historical narratives, then, never are "just" history. There always is a great deal at stake for narrator and readers, always much to gain and lose in power and meaning.[5]

In other words, he is calling for the dis-covery of those stories, places, and voices that have been excluded from the grand narratives. He is not arguing against historical narratives, but against the way historical narratives (macro-narratives) have been developed. Since the modernist/colonial agenda guided the establishment of narratives as universal, it is not a matter, then, of exchanging the stories and players in the narratives. The dis-covery of voices and stories challenges the content of the narratives but also its universal character. In this sense, these dis-covered voices should offer new perspectives that transform the historical discipline by promoting openness to difference and dismantling the universal aura of a particular narrative.[6] While he acknowledges, as I have mentioned before, that the most recent major surveys have dealt with the issue of diversity, the main characters and the storyline are still the same, which was Roger D. Hatch's argument on the nonrevision of the subject matter of the standard narrative.

The essays in this book go beyond a mere introduction of new topics and themes to actually providing new interpretative lenses and paradigms. The authors not only reconfigured the way to write history; they used new paradigms to uncover silences rather than revisit the old themes and motifs. These essays, as Steve McKinzie

[5] Tweed, "Introduction," 2.

[6] My use of the verb "should" is conscious since I believe that many times the dis-covered voices just want to replace the existing ones and reproduce the exercise of power. If these "new" voices do not search for the supremacy of difference as an overarching idea, society will be still guided by the colonial imaginary. The only difference would be the people in power.

acknowledged, lack cohesiveness as a whole, but I believe this proves the discontinuities within the writing of history and that it is in those discontinuities, in those spaces, where hidden stories are found. It is a matter of looking for them and exposing them.[7] On the other hand, McKinzie's point cannot just be disregarded because in order to provide an alternative to the canon (a counter-discourse), historians have to be aware of the connections between the discontinuities of their particular projects. It is not a matter of constructing a new macro-narrative based on progress and continuity, but it is essential to the process of confrontation and the process of dis-covery to make associations among the silences. If these connections are not made, the project would be limited to a trivial postmodern enterprise that deconstructs in order to expose particularity but does not take the time to construct on the bases of the many relationships between particularities. Silences are usually connected through the history of colonialism.

Another anthology that confronts the canon is David G. Hackett's *Religion and American Culture: A Reader.*[8] In the book's introduction, Hackett states:

> Today the study of American religion continues to move away from an older European American, male, middle-class, northeastern, Protestant narrative concerned primarily with churches and theology and toward a multicultural tale of Native Americans, African Americans, Catholics, Jews and other groups. Many of these new studies cut across boundaries of gender, class, and region, and pay particular attention to popular religion.[9]

For Hackett this is the current status of the field, and the collection of essays in the book reflects this condition. Hackett acknowledges that the field is undergoing revisions, many of which I have addressed, but he emphasizes the importance of the expansions of subject matter during the 1990s:

[7] Steve McKinzie, "Saints and Revisionists: Refashioning the American Religious Narrative," *Cross Currents* 48, no. 1 (1998): 104.

[8] David G. Hackett, ed., *Religion and American Culture: A Reader* (New York: Routledge, 1995).

[9] David G. Hackett, "Introduction," in Hackett, *Religion and American Culture*, ix.

> Regional religious stories of the West and the South are coming into view. Native American religious history, non-existent as a field until the 1980s, is an exciting and rapidly emerging new discipline. Dramatic revisions are being made in our understanding of the African American religious past. Mormons, Masons, Pentecostals, ethnic Catholics, sunbelt Jews, followers of Islam, Asian religions, and Haitian Vodou are now on the scene. Attention is being given to the relationship between religion and commercial culture. The complex view of women in today's women's studies is echoed in new works on women across class and racial lines. In many of these studies we can see a new interest in ritual and ceremony.[10]

Hackett introduced the richness and diversity of the field to justify that it is not time for a textbook, since it would not be able to grasp this diversity, but time for "an anthology that gives clear voice to these new studies."[11] This anthology does exactly that.

The essays in *Religion and American Culture: A Reader* cover a vast terrain of topics, themes, and paradigms, from Native American religion to Mormonism, from nationalism to popular religion, and from magic to Haitian Vodou. Most of the groups that were silenced by the canon can see part of their history one way or another in these essays. Thus, this anthology provides these groups with a historical voice. However, as was the case in *Retelling U.S. Religious History,* the articles in this collection run the danger of falling into the sea of particularities in which the dominant hegemonic voice will perpetuate its control. Although this collection definitively confronts and exposes the canon, some silences are still maintained. I will just mention two of them, which are also true for *Retelling U.S. Religious History.* The first has to do with the inclusion of race and gender as criteria of analysis, not just as topics. Gender and race are clearly used in several of the essays, but most of them incorporate gender and race because they become the themes of the project, not because they are an intrinsic part of the project's theoretical scaffold. With class this is even clearer because it is almost always mentioned and analyzed in superficial ways, and the analysis is inevitably organized from the perspective of the dominant class. An example of this is Tamar Frankiel's

[10] Hackett, "Introduction," ix.
[11] Hackett, "Introduction," x.

"California Dreams," which is a history of the West from the perspective of the groups that moved to this region, not from the perspective of the people who already lived there.[12] While issues of race and gender are discussed, the subjects of the story are still the same—men, white people, and dominant class, respectively.

The second silence has to do with the lack of the representation of Latinas/os as historical subjects. Allan Figueroa Deck's essay on the way Evangelicalism/Pentecostalism challenges the Catholic Church within the Latina/o community is the only essay in which the Latina/o is the subject of the story.[13] Interestingly enough, in parts II and III, which cover the periods 1750–1865 and 1865–1945, respectively, there is no article that focuses on the imperial character of the expansion of the United States. Frankiel deals with the missionary activity in the West, but from the perspective of the missionaries, not from the perspective of the recipients of that activity. Thus, the presence of Latinas/os in the larger discussion of U.S. religious history can be seen as peripheral or "new," since Figueroa Deck's article discusses more of the contemporary situation. But these setbacks aside, both collections are the best resources for seeing the directions in which the field is moving and needs to continue to move. The presence of "new" voices opens the door for the incorporation of other voices, and that is the direction for which I am arguing.

Unlike *Retelling U.S. Religious History* and *Religion and American Culture: A Reader,* other collections published in the 1990s, which have brought to the table new approaches and perspectives, have not confronted the traditional and modern/colonial character of U.S. religious historiography. One example of this kind of work is the collection *New Directions in American Religious History,* edited by Harry S. Stout and D. G. Hart.[14] The articles in this anthology were collected from a 1993 conference of the same name. The articles were written following these guidelines:

> Given the decisive shifts in historiography from mainline to sideline in the past twenty years, the conference planners asked the

[12] Tamar Frankiel, "California Dreams," in Hackett, *Religion and American Culture,* 211–25.

[13] Allan Figueroa Deck, "The Challenge of Evangelical/Pentecostal Christianity to Hispanic Catholicism," in Hackett, *Religion and American Culture,* 462–77.

[14] See Harry S. Stout and D. G. Hart, eds., *New Directions in American Religious History* (New York: Oxford University Press, 1997).

> participants to think of the new groups they are studying and the histories they yield in dialectical tension with the old Protestant mainline histories, thus bringing the old "Church History"—Protestant centered and intellectually based—into dialogue with the new, non-mainline-centered and socially based "religious history."[15]

Although this premise conveys hope to the readers that the articles in the book will serve as groundbreaking material, both in content and method, the book falls short of this objective. While it is acknowledged that this is a period of growth and transition in the study of religion in the United States, the essays in the book do not provide new material to work with as much as new perspectives on the same old topics and themes.

The authors in *New Directions in American History* looked at the old stories and introduced a "new" way of rethinking and rewriting them. Again, there is no intent of writing new stories, because as Laura F. Winner says, "Stout and Hart are more concerned with refining the stories we have."[16] The authors wanted to create a change in the way religious history in the United States was being told, so they took the already existing topics and themes (Puritanism, voluntarism, U.S. African American religion, Catholicism, Judaism, and others) and worked on them, trying to find out how they fit into the present condition of the study of religion in the United States. The new perspectives should be taken into consideration if those topics and themes are going to be re-examined, but besides the discussion about the use of sociology and the new social history in the first chapter and a large number of works cited within the different essays, the book does not offer new paths to follow. Paul Boyer makes an excellent critique by asserting that this book does not take into consideration the changes in the religious life of the United States. This book has not paid attention to the religious and ethnic diversity present in today's society. Boyer establishes the importance of different groups in the development of the social, political, and economic structures of the United States. He points out:

> With a few exceptions, this book addresses specific sectors of *white American Protestant* history. One would hardly guess from this

[15] Harry S. Stout and D. G. Hart, "Introduction," in Stout and Hart, *New Directions*, 4–5.

[16] Winner, "Retold, Redirected," 20.

> volume that Hispanics (mainly Catholic, with a strong evangelical and Pentecostalist admixture) will soon overtake blacks as the nation's largest minority; that Islam is poised to supplant Judaism as America's second largest religion after Christianity; that Pentecostalism has been the most vital and dynamic force in the twentieth-century American religious life; that Quakers, Unitarians, and Episcopalians, while relatively few in number, have played outsized roles in American social, intellectual, political (and military) history; that America has spawned new religions that today enroll many millions worldwide, including Mormonism, Christian Science, Jehovah's Witness, and Seventh-Day Adventist; that televangelist Billy Graham was this century's most influential American Christian leader worldwide; or that heterodox religious innovators, from the Fox sisters and William Miller to the latest New Age guru or Bible-prophecy popularizer, have profoundly shaped the American religious scene.[17]

It is a matter of reviewing the book to be able to see that this initiative failed to grasp most of the dimensions that can shift the nature and direction in religious history in the United States.

The second section, following an essay on historiography in the first part, is dedicated to essays that deal with regions, focusing on Protestantism in New England, Canada, and the South, leaving the Southwest and West without any kind of treatment. These regions are seen as empty land ready to be conquered, and the people living there as objects of a missionary enterprise, not as actual subjects with a historical voice or consciousness. This follows Turner's frontier thesis. Of course, the treatment of the South is only based on the black/white relationship. The third section is dedicated to stages of Protestantism (revivals, American revolution, and voluntarism) and the fourth to Protestantism and the mainstream (ethnicity-WASP, economy, urbanism, gender, missions, and experience). It is not until the last part that other non-white Protestants are introduced in the book and only three communities are represented, African Americans, Catholics, and Jews. This book follows a traditional approach to the study of religion in the United States, giving priority to the

[17] Paul Boyer, "Testimony Time: Historians Reflect on Current Issues in American Religious History," *Evangelical Studies Bulletin* 15, no. 3 (1998): 4 (emphasis in original).

white-Protestant (Puritan) experience and leaving on the outside the discussion the examination of the Others. John Higham's article, "Ethnicity and American Protestants: Collective Identity in the Mainstream," serves as the best example of this kind of marginalization.[18] While the author talks about ethnicity, he does not open the discussion to communities outside the non-Spanish-speaking European immigrants, leaving them, again, without a historical voice.

I argue that this collection, as the others, serves, intentionally or unintentionally, to preserve the status quo and the normative character of the dominant discourse (the canon in U.S. religious historiography). The only difference with these surveys is that now macro-narrative has been replaced by micro-narratives, but the standard narrative is still the dominant discourse. Stories and voices are still silenced and covered, and the historical voice of the people on the borderlands is still excluded from the discourse. In this regard, Harry Stout and R. M. Taylor state that "historians do not need to pursue ever-new topics so much as they need to relate their work to broader, theoretical concerns."[19] Contrary to Stout and Taylor's point, I argue that historians should not treat the theoretical concerns and the new topics separately since they need to enter into a dialectical relationship through which they may reshape each other constantly. This dialectical relationship is essential in the project of addressing exclusion and silencing by opening spaces to new voices and new interpretative paradigms that ultimately should develop discourses based on difference.

I would like to mention and briefly examine three more anthologies that follow the same path as *New Directions in American Religious History*. The first is *American Church History: A Reader*, edited by Henry Warner Bowden and P. C. Kemeny, which contains thirty-three articles divided into five parts.[20] This collection includes the same topics on which the standard narrative is based. Even in the second part, dedicated to ethnicity, while five articles focus their attention on WASP communities, only one examines the black

[18] John Higham, "Ethnicity and American Protestants: Collective Identity in the Mainstream," in Stout and Hart, *New Directions*, 239–59.

[19] Harry S. Stout and R. M. Taylor, "Studies of Religion in American Society: The State of the Art," in Stout and Hart, *New Directions*, 36.

[20] Henry Warner Bowden and P. C. Kemeny, eds., *American Church History: A Reader* (Nashville: Abingdon, 1998).

experience.[21] The presence of articles dealing with issues of race and gender and with non-Protestant communities is a positive sign, but even in those the standard narrative is left unexamined and the topic is still treated as a particular issue, outside the dominant discourse. The issues of race and gender are not an integral part of the theoretical scaffold of analysis. The absence of Native American, Asian American, and Latina/o communities is obvious, so these groups are once again marginalized and left out of the religious historical discourse.

Another compilation of essays that continued with the same approach is *Religion in American History: A Reader.*[22] The editors, Jon Butler and Harry S. Stout, set out to prepare this reader as a way of provoking the interest of students and other scholars in religion within U.S. society. They included primary sources from the three major periods into which the book is divided: colonial, nineteenth century, and twentieth century, as well as secondary material by religious historians, some old material and some new material. They wanted to show the changes in the field through the inclusion of different material from different times, arguing that

> A great historiographical transition has occurred over the past generation—the transition from "intellectual history" of major philosophers and theologians and a history of "public events" in churches and denominations that dominated early scholarship, to the "social history" of "ordinary people" that characterizes recent historiography. Neither of these traditions is "right" or "wrong," rather, they complement each other; when they are taken together, they greatly enrich and deepen our understanding of religion in American life.[23]

The historiographical transition is clearly present in the selection of essays; the problem resides in the themes and topics discussed in the essays. While they openly state, "We have tried to give voice

[21] Martin E. Marty's "Ethnicity: The Skeleton of Religion in America" is the first article in this section. The specific content of the essay will be discussed in the next section.

[22] Jon Butler and Harry S. Stout, eds., *Religion in American History: A Reader* (New York: Oxford University Press, 1998).

[23] Jon Butler and Harry S. Stout, "Introduction," in Butler and Stout, *Religion in American History*, 3.

to the largest possible range of participants: women as well as men; African Americans as well as European Americans; 'ordinary people' as well as more 'elite' public figures,"[24] the themes and topics still reflect a dependency on the standard narrative. The inclusion of certain groups, certain Others such as Native Americans, African Americans, Jews, women, and Catholics, is definitely a step forward. Yet the argument and subject matter that lie beneath the purpose of the book remain the same as in the dominant discourse. The subjects of the stories are still the same. An example is that in the section about the nineteenth century, no article is dedicated to the social, political, and religious situation in the Southwest, leaving the importance of the Mexican-U.S. War outside the discourse. The same can be said about the last section on the twentieth century. During that time period, the issues of non-European immigration and Nativism were vital but are not introduced in the essays. Power is still exercised by the dominant group.

This perpetuation of power is clear in the collection *Perspectives on American Religion and Culture.*[25] In this anthology there is a section on race and ethnicity that consists of three articles. The first one discusses the relationship between blacks and whites, the second offers new perspectives on African American religion, and the third examines different Native American movements and their writings. Obviously, this collection incorporates new motifs in other sections, especially an incisive article on the American West by Laurie Maffly-Kipp at the beginning of the book,[26] but the section on race and ethnicity portrays the way the standard narrative has opened itself up from the inside to give certain spaces to the subaltern without threatening its control. The African American perspectives once again are given spaces in order to continue with the establishment of a black/white paradigm, while the Native American perspective is an oasis among many other traditional themes and topics, like Jonathan Edwards, Revivalism, Catholicism, and Puritanism. Even when

[24] Butler and Stout, "Introduction," 3.

[25] Peter Williams, ed., *Perspectives on American Religion and Culture* (Malden, Mass.: Blackwell, 1999).

[26] Laurie Maffly-Kipp, "Historicizing Religion in the American West," in Williams, *Perspectives on American Religion and Culture.* This is an essay that examines the West and introduces the contact and exchange between groups, specifically in California, during the immigration of Chinese to this portion of the nation.

issues such as gender are included, the standard narrative is not challenged because they are treated from the dominant perspective. In conclusion, the content of these two collections reveals that the standard narrative is still the dominant discourse within the field, no longer in a macro-narrative style but in a micro-narrative one.

In any case, it is important to establish that U.S. religious historiography has benefited from these anthologies since they introduced new material or re-evaluated the old. The different projects available serve as indicators of the many ventures in which scholars in the field are engaged. At the same time, some of them show that the standard narrative is still a used paradigm. Tweed's and Hackett's collections provide significant optimism about the future of the field, but for now it is important not to avoid confrontation with projects that do not serve the purpose of revising the dominant discourse, but on the other hand serve in the legitimation of the standard narrative and the modern project. This examination of some anthologies in U.S. religious history provides a clear look at the direction these two kinds of projects take. The last two examples have not produced any alternative knowledge to modernity, but instead have become part of the colonial project. Even when they have set out to include more participants, they have not been able to explore the discontinuities, as in, for example, Tweed's and Hackett's works. Mark A. Noll, in the passage quoted earlier, mentioned that there is still no clarity regarding the inclusion of those people who were left out of the standard narrative in the story of Christianity in the United States. After analyzing the "new" micro-narratives and the projects they represent, it is clear that the problem resides in the lack of critique of the scaffold that sustains the standard narrative, that being the modern project.

The inclusion of a critique of the modern project would actually expand and redefine the understanding of pluralism in U.S. religious historiography. Although some of these texts help unmask the dominant discourse (canon) as exclusive because it leaves on the borderlands other religious expressions outside the mainline Protestant world, David Daniels argues that "a serious critique of the modern project and its constriction of alternative narrative is necessary before a new direction in historiographical narrative is actually possible."[27] He argues that the last revisions of the standard narrative

[27] David Daniels, "Teaching the History of U.S. Christianity in a Global Perspective," *Theological Education* 29, no. 2 (1993): 99.

dealt with the making of religious pluralism but still supported the modern project. So Daniels goes on to propose,

> To revise this thesis and move toward a globalized interpretation, the making of religious pluralism needs to shift from procedural discourse which distinguishes pluralities, majorities, and minorities, to ecological discourse of post-modern musings. For example, the making of religious pluralism might be re-defined in terms of heterogeneity instead of homogeneity.[28]

In this sense, it is important to mention that in order to construct a functional counter-discourse, one has to follow the path to which collections like Tweed's and Hackett's point. A critique of the modern character, embedded in the foundation of U.S. religious historiography, is required. Although I agree with Daniels' argument on the revision of religious pluralism, I feel that a thorough revision of racial pluralism is needed as well in order to deconstruct the entire field of studies because revisions within it are scarce. Thus, postmodern musings are needed within this field as well.

THE SCAFFOLD OF A BLACK/WHITE PARADIGM

Up to this point, I have given a summary of the literature available in the field of U.S. religious history, providing a critique of the standard narrative (modern project) embedded in most of the literature. I have discussed the issue of religious pluralism, but the aspect that has not been fully addressed in the study of religion in the United States is the racial issue. One reason for the lack of emphasis on this issue is the scholars' assumption of a black/white paradigm that leaves out of the analysis the people in the middle of this spectrum. "Historically, race in the United States has been perceived as a black-white issue."[29] As I suggested before, most of the work in the field has been willing to include the study of African American religion, although Roger D. Hatch's article provides the condition of that inclusion. In this regard, this inclusion has created and solidified a paradigm to deal with the issues of race and ethnicity. The issue of race is only

[28] Daniels, "Teaching the History," 97.

[29] Teresa Chávez-Sauceda, "Race, Religion, and la Raza: An Exploration of the Racialization of Latinos in the United States and the Role of the Protestant Church," in *Protestantes/Protestants: Hispanic Christianity within Mainline Traditions*, ed. David Maldonado Jr. (Nashville: Abingdon, 1999), 178.

examined as a binary opposition between black and white. Every topic or issue is studied, interpreted, and analyzed based on the relationship between these two groups. In this paradigm the white still has control over the voice of the black and still dominates the discourse, but the inclusion, although peripheral, of a black voice has given the white a sense of accomplishment since it appears as if the standard narrative has been revised and opened to diversity. Thus, as I argued before, the subject of the story remains the same; it does not change. As a matter of fact, the standard narrative is still closed, not only to the black subject, but especially to the voices outside (or in the middle) of the black/white paradigm.

At the same time, the issue of ethnicity has only been dealt with as far is it pertains to European immigration.[30] As Charles H. Long affirms, "In short, a great deal of the writings and discussions on the topic of American religion has been consciously or unconsciously ideological, serving to enhance, justify, and render sacred the history of European immigrants in this land."[31] Ethnicity, in this sense, is only seen through male WASP lenses. Although U.S. Native Americans, U.S. Latinas/os, and U.S. Asian Americans are mentioned in some of the literature, the issue of ethnicity enters the discussion if it relates to the condition of the European immigrants and their relationship with the subaltern.

In order to provide reference and prove my point, I will turn now to the discussion of several articles that have dealt with the issues of race and ethnicity in this field. In them, these two points about race and ethnicity will be made clear. In 1972 Martin E. Marty published

[30] The existence of a black/white paradigm has not only been based on the color of the skin but also on the actual construction of whiteness. The issue of ethnicity is discussed here precisely because of its relationship to the construction of whiteness. While in the history of the United States there were periods in which Europeans marginalized other European newcomers (the Irish and Italians, for example) for their religious beliefs and culture, among other things, throughout time the differences between these groups have been displaced by the construction of a particular identity, being "American." This construction is based on, but not defined by, the color of the skin. So, in this sense it is important to understand the treatment of the issue of ethnicity because it should be seen as outside of the realm of the black/white paradigm, but as an essential piece for the development of this paradigm.

[31] Charles H. Long, "A New Look at American Religion," in *The Writing of American Religious History*, ed. Martin E. Marty (Munich: K.G. Saur, 1992), 87.

the article "Ethnicity: The Skeleton of Religion in America," later published under the title "Peoples: The Thickness of Pluralism" as part of a book.[32] Marty exposes the importance of ethnicity in the understanding of religion in the United States to the point that he establishes "ethnicity as the skeleton of religion in America."[33] He talks about five major types of interpretation of religion in the United States based on the issue of ethnicity: 1) the secular—less religion (spirituality) in a society moving toward secularization; 2) the private—religion is part of the individual's private life and has no relationship with the social; 3) the pluralist—the differences were left aside for the communal identification; 4) the denominational—denominations are the basis of interpretation; and 5) the common-religious—there is a common civil religion in which everyone participates. Marty finds that none of these five modes of interpretation can be applied to non-WASP groups and thus "racial and ethnic particularity deserves compensatory interest and inquiry."[34] For him this effort "should help historians deal more adequately with the faded, predestined, tragic and even violent elements in religion in America."[35]

This article is important because of its critiques of the standard narrative. Of course, the author is not explicit in his critique. However, Marty exposes the standard narrative when he states, "The themes of WASP ethnicity and superiority which had been explicit in the nineteenth century became implicit and taken for granted in the twentieth."[36] Equally, he acknowledges that the particularism in the WASP themes have been shown as universalism, which as I argue is one of the major characteristics of the modern project embedded in the canon of U.S. religious historiography. The author wants to open the interpretation beyond the five established modes of analysis in order to provide a better understanding of the situation of religion in the United States and its relationship to ethnicity. The

[32] Martin E. Marty, "Peoples: The Thickness of Pluralism," in *Religion and Republic: The American Circumstance* (Boston: Beacon, 1987), 227–47; first published as "Ethnicity: The Skeleton of Religion in America," *Church History* 41 (1972): 5–21.

[33] Marty, "Peoples," 231.

[34] Marty, "Peoples," 244.

[35] Marty, "Peoples," 245.

[36] Marty, "Peoples," 246.

problem resides in that even with a call to openness and some kind of revision, Marty does not offer alternatives or specific clues on how this could be achieved. Hence the skeleton, although acknowledged, was still left inside the closet and the WASP themes continued to dominate the standard narrative. Thus, it is important to take up Marty's challenge and construct alternatives.

Three years after Marty wrote his proposal for a better understanding of ethnicity, Harry S. Stout published his article "Ethnicity: The Vital Center of Religion in America."[37] Stout, as does Marty, calls for a more rigorous study of the relationship between ethnicity and religion in the United States and what he calls ethnoreligion, since he argues that "the history of American churches cannot be described solely in terms of the frontier, urbanization, or denominations but must recognize the centrality of ethnicity in American religious life."[38] Even with this call, however, his argument is a step back from Marty's challenge. Stout argues for the presence of a three-stage model in understanding the development of an ethnoreligion in the United States. The first stage is the "immigrant" phase in which different ethnic groups come together "around an amalgam of ecclesiastical and national origins."[39] The second stage is represented with the people's allegiance to different groups (Protestant-Catholic-Jew-African American).[40] The third phase corresponds to the culmination of the second, where the different groups merge into a common sentiment of what it is to be an American. Stout writes,

[37] Harry S. Stout, "Ethnicity: The Vital Center of Religion in America," *Ethnicity* 2 (1975): 204–24.

[38] Stout, "Ethnicity," 220.

[39] Stout, "Ethnicity," 207.

[40] This model, without the black presence, is proposed in Will Herberg, *Protestant-Catholic-Jew: An Essay in American Religious Sociology* (Garden City, N.Y.: Anchor, 1955). Stout added the black component to Herberg's three-party model. This four-party model did not reflect the differences within the different groups nor was it inclusive of the other religious groups in the United States. In other words, it corresponded only to a sector of society and supported the standard narrative by homogenizing plurality. It may seem as if two of these are religious groups in essence and not ethnic (Protestant and Catholic) but even these groups represent particular ethnic communities (Catholics—Irish, Italians, eastern Europeans, among others; Protestants—Anglo-Saxons).

> An intricate religious montage emerges in which plurality and consensus are simultaneously visible in the American Way. The previously disparate ethnoreligion exists in a state of mutual toleration in the third stage precisely because they have been replaced by the American culture religion; a national ethnoreligion is the final product.[41]

This culmination of the process serves only the subject who characterizes what is exactly "the American Way." It does not benefit those who do not play a role in the construction of what is the "American Way." The subaltern is left without a voice in the construction of a system of which they are later on "compelled" (forced somehow) to be part.[42]

Stout's article does not open the doors for a new understanding of the relationship between religion and ethnicity in the United States but mostly perpetuates the traditional paradigms that, as Marty acknowledges, "apply appropriately only to the white and largely generalized Protestant academic circles where they originated."[43] In his conclusion, Stout acknowledges the presence of exceptions to the model without identifying them particularly. Instead, he characterizes these "prominent" exceptions as "the sects, societies, and individuals who failed to thrive among a compelling and dominant ethnic religion in America."[44] This characterization is an obvious sign of a nativist attitude against the subaltern in society, in which those who do not want to be part of a dominant system are marginalized no matter how exclusive and oppressive that system is. While the author states that the paradigm he is proposing is not to be taken as the only one and that "the model rejects simplistic generalizations ordered around concepts of assimilation or pluralism because both dimensions are present in the ethnic process in different phases,"[45] he does exactly that, generalizing and grouping without actually questioning the allegiances to a system or *the* system itself. The worst thing is that this grouping process tries to erase

[41] Stout, "Ethnicity," 216.

[42] R. Laurence Moore's argument fits here perfectly because he argued against this construction since he believed that those others, the outsiders, are intrinsic parts in the development of an identity.

[43] Marty, "Peoples," 244.

[44] Stout, "Ethnicity," 219.

[45] Stout, "Ethnicity," 220.

the particularities of each group to the benefit, again, of those who construct the group, "the American Way of Life." This article points out the interrelationships between ethnicity and religion while insisting on a particular way of looking at those interrelationships from the point of view of those in power, not from the point of view of the subaltern.

More than two decades later, John Higham revisited this issue of ethnicity with particular concern about its relationship to mainstream Protestantism.[46] He begins his essay with a bibliographical argument in which he details most of the literature and paradigms available in order to understand ethnicity and its connection to religion. Later on, he provides a brief comparison between Moore's *Religious Outsiders and the Making of Americans* and Stout's article "Ethnicity," which I discussed above. Higham's interest is to explore the characteristics of an American Protestant identity that, he acknowledges, has been constructed by many. For him, "The pursuit of a generalized Protestant identity can be studied anew by examining Stout's framework in the context of Moore's pluralistic insights."[47] Higham examines the literature in the field of U.S. history in order to study the meaning of Protestantism in connection to ethnicity in the process of the development of the nation. He concludes that Protestantism cannot be defined based on the boundaries of a single ethnic group, since that model has failed, but should be defined based on ethnic plurality.[48] Higham does not provide a new vision but concentrates on the critique of the existing paradigm or the lack of one. Even the critique is not complete because, as I argued before, the WASP dominant discourse is still embedded in Higham's argument. His point of reference is the Anglo-Protestant northeast, leaving once again the rest of the continent without a historical consciousness. The absence of a concrete proposal ultimately benefits those in power because there is no alternative to their scaffolds (the modern project) and their use of them in order to marginalize and colonize. On the contrary, the new critiques and projects, as did Higham's, have served to solidify the standard narrative because it has revised itself from the inside, not from the outside, perpetuating the exercise of power as any other modern/colonial discourse.

[46] Higham, "Ethnicity and American Protestants."

[47] Higham, "Ethnicity and American Protestants," 245.

[48] Higham, "Ethnicity and American Protestants," 255.

The construction of a black/white paradigm has served U.S. religious historiography as a means of internal revision in the interpretation of racial/ethnic relationships within religious experience in the United States. While many voices have come to the forefront of the discussion, the counter-discourses have not developed a clear critique and confrontation of this paradigm. They have not gone far enough. Tweed's and Hackett's are two examples of projects that confront the traditional canon but lack a solid critique of this paradigm and an inclusion of race as an integral interpretative criterion. Scholarship is moving that direction, but until this is achieved it is important to continue the process of confrontation and the deconstruction of this paradigm, which still dominates the writing of U.S. religious history. The three-party system opened the canon to two non-Protestant groups, Catholicism and Judaism, in order to give the impression that the Protestant-Puritan perspective no longer dominated the standard narrative. It is clear from the literature analyzed in this chapter that it was this Protestant-Puritan perspective that defined those two groups and selected the spaces they were going to occupy. These groups had a voice inasmuch as they contributed to that "American Way of Life." Dissenting voices are considered exceptions and enter the texts as footnotes. The same happens with the inclusion of the black perspective, and Roger D. Hatch's article illustrates this reality. This racial/ethnic paradigm sustains the standard narrative by including chapters on the religious experience of African Americans but keeping the male WASP-dominated discourse at the center. African American voices have been recuperated and many of their stories have been uncovered, but other Others have been relegated to the borderlands and their voices are kept silenced and covered. This black/white paradigm has built two valid poles. The groups that do not fit in either of the poles are boxed into one of the poles or just left out.

I have explored pieces of U.S. religious historiography in order to exemplify how it works as a colonial enterprise. In this chapter, understanding that there are other silences I have not addressed, I have focused, mainly, on the issue of race. Historians like Ahlstrom, Gaustad, Marty, and Handy introduced pluralism to their narrative, and scholars like Moore built upon these arguments in order to construct an alternative discourse. Following that same path, other projects, like Tweed's and Hackett's, increased the critique of the standard narrative and provided an even more open discourse. Even in the last few years, works from both within and outside the field continue to challenge the established paradigms, especially as these bring new theoretical and methodological approaches to the concept of religion and the study of religious communities.[49] However, this process needs to go further in its analysis to deconstruct the paradigms that hold together the canon; indeed, some of the new projects do not seek confrontation, only new perspectives without deconstructing the established paradigms. In this sense, I find that the goal should not only be to uncover the silences, but also to give those silenced voices the opportunity to speak as subjects, and for that confrontation needs to happen. The breaking down of the system not only provides openness to these new voices, as many revisions have, but it presents the opportunity of recreating theories and paradigms that are actually opened to constant change as more voices are incorporated. Latinas/os as subaltern agents break the established paradigm, and Latina/o religious history is responsible for bringing these voices to the forefront in order to deconstruct not only this paradigm, but also the traditional historical discourses within U.S. religious history.

[49] These recent theoretical and methodological approaches problematize not simply the concept of religion but also the way one should look at religious beliefs and the communities of faith. They deal with modernity/secularity, immigrations, displacements, the material aspects of religion, among others, but mostly they all deal with the everyday aspect of religion, the experiencing of religion, which is something I address later in the book as I explore lived religions. See Nancy T. Ammerman, ed., *Everyday Religion: Observing Modern Religious Lives* (New York: Oxford University Press, 2006); Thomas A. Tweed, *Crossing and Dwelling: A Theory of Religion* (Cambridge, Mass.: Harvard University Press, 2008); and Manuel A. Vasquez, *More Than a Belief: A Materialist Theory of Religion* (New York: Oxford University Press, 2010).

PART II

A LOOK AT LATINA/O RELIGIOUS HISTORIOGRAPHY

This book is about the construction of subversive counter-discourses within the historical field. Latina/o religious historiography can be considered a subversive enterprise since it uncovers themes, voices, and stories hidden by the dominant U.S. religious historical discourses examined in the first part. While the field of Latina/o religious history has been growing in the last decade, it is still marginalized and absent from major academic institutions and projects that still see this literature as a footnote within the larger narratives. A simple look at the literature within this field is enough to see the diversity of material scholars have been able to put at the forefront of their research that may have been left outside the traditional narratives about U.S. religious history. They are mostly guided by denominational, regional, or national interest and the themes of marginalization, paternalism, prejudice (racial, religious, and ethnic), and "Americanization," themes that are present and exposed in most of the literature. On the other hand, a deeper look at these multiple projects provides an opportunity to understand what approaches and paradigms scholars have been using and developing as they read the data and write their narratives. This second part of the book is interested in this deeper analysis.

The field of Latina/o religious history has been divided into two major areas, Catholic histories and Protestant histories. While I explore each area separately in the next two chapters, it is important to acknowledge that both have followed similar developments. In the first stages of the field, the interest of authors (scholars and church leaders alike) was to find faces, names, and stories of Latina/o people—especially Mexicans and Mexican Americans—in order to prove the presence of this community within the larger religious communities. Once some of these stories had been uncovered, there was an interest in proving the agency of the Latinas/os by positioning them not merely as recipients of missionary enterprises or paternalistic attitudes but as subjects of their own stories. In many cases the setback of this approach was that while these works provided glimpses of that agency, it was still seen through the perspective of those in power and not through the people themselves. Over the last decade or so, the literature has been able to show the agency of these communities through the eyes of the people since much of this work has been developed through ethnographical and other sociocultural historical approaches. It is within this stage, where we find ourselves today, that I feel we should be talking about methods and theories of analysis that would increase the capacity of the field to create projects that follow a postcolonizing perspective, the topic I will be discussing in the third part.

In the next two chapters, I look at some of the major literature within the field of U.S. Latina/o religious history, not all, in order to examine the production of these projects. My analysis consists in exploring the methods and theories being used by scholars within this field as they construct their discourses. I will not, of course, examine each of the available projects, nor am I interested in an in-depth review of this literature as it pertains to its content. An analysis of the approaches and hermeneutical keys behind the construction of the discourses allows us to understand the trajectory and state of the field in order to attempt to move it forward through the development of new theories and methods. Each chapter includes a historiographical survey of the literature that offers an overview of the development of the respective area within the field of U.S. Latina/o religious history. After that survey, I offer an analysis of the major trends and paradigms. It is important to restate that I focus my analysis on historical material, so many other theological and sociological works that are crucial in the development of the larger field of Latina/o religious studies are not examined here. While I recognize the importance of these studies, I wanted to concentrate my own analysis within the field of history, even if I know that the boundaries of these disciplines are fluid, especially as pertains to Latina/o religions.

3 CATHOLIC HISTORIES

Spanish-speaking Catholics have been continuously presente *in what is now the continental United States for almost twice as long as the nation has existed.*

—Timothy Matovina and Gerald E. Poyo, "Introduction," in *¡Presente!*, xv

While the actual field of Latina/o Catholic history has been slowly developing in the last two decades, Latina/o Catholicism has been explored from multiple perspectives both from within and outside the academic world.[1] In many cases, the normative narratives of U.S. Catholicism have marginalized these examinations and labeled them as contextual, as if they were not part of the larger Catholic experience in the United States. "While Hispanics were the first Catholic (as well as first European) inhabitants to establish settlements in territories now under U.S. control, for much of U.S. history Hispanics have constituted a relatively small and frequently overlooked group within U.S. Catholicism."[2] This is one of

[1] For a collection of much of the research done within this area of studies, see Kenneth G. Davis, Eduardo C. Fernández, and Verónica Méndez, eds., *United States Hispanic Catholics: Trends and Works, 1990–2000* (Scranton, Pa.: University of Scranton Press, 2002). Much of the discourse has been related to theology, spirituality, and ritual and ministry studies, while historical studies have been lacking.

[2] Timothy Matovina and Gerald E. Poyo, "Introduction," in *¡Presente!: U.S. Latino Catholics from Colonial Origins to the Present*, ed. Timothy Matovina and Gerald E. Poyo (Maryknoll, N.Y.: Orbis Books, 2000), xv.

the reasons this field is still in its building stages. Even though the production has grown over the last decade, there is still much work to explore, and the lack of emphasis and focus provided by the larger academic setting has made it hard to build a solid field.

At the same time, scholars within this field have always confronted difficulties within their work. In 1994 Jay P. Dolan and Allan Figueroa Deck argued that, "The dilemma facing contemporary students of U.S. Hispanic Catholic history is two-fold: 1) a lack of easy access to many of the primary sources such as parish and diocesan archives or the files of influential apostolic movements and organizations; and 2) a dearth of scholarly monographs on the vast range of topics relevant to the history of Hispanics in the United States Catholic Church."[3] While this dilemma is still present, the use of new approaches to the study of these histories has allowed scholars to move the field forward. Here lies my interest.

In this chapter I take a quick look at some of the major historical works in the area in order to assess the way these discourses have been constructed. I am not interested in analyzing the multiple themes and topics that have guided these narratives, but in the process and the scaffold used in their construction. In the first section, I do a historiographical survey of the major works in the field. Although I recognize that there are many important articles, theses, dissertations, and nonscholarly works within this field, I focus my analysis on academic books, understanding that this approach limits the scope of my analysis. In the second section, I highlight the major approaches used by scholars in order to construct their historical discourses and facilitate the evolution of the field, in order to compare them with the ones used within Latina/o Protestantism in the United States,which I explore in the next chapter, and contrast them with theories and methods within the larger field of U.S. religious history.

HISTORIOGRAPHICAL SURVEY

In 1983, commissioned by CEHILA (Comisión para el Estudio de la Historia de la Iglesia en América Latina), Moises Sandoval edited *Fronteras: A History of the Latin American Church in the USA since*

[3] Jay P. Dolan and Allan Figueroa Deck, "Introduction," in *Hispanic Catholic Culture in the U.S.: Issues and Concerns*, ed. Jay P. Dolan and Allan Figueroa Deck (Notre Dame: University of Notre Dame Press, 1994), 1.

1523.[4] This project, an anthology of articles, came to fill a vacuum within the literature of the Catholic history of the United States. It was constructed following the CEHILA model of scholarship, which is doing *historia desde abajo* (history from below) from the perspective of liberation. As Ricardo Ramirez argues in the preface, "CEHILA looks at history from the point of view of the oppressed in their quest for liberation," and once history is done from this perspective it "concentrates on the victories and defeats of a people seeking to be full human beings."[5] Scholars, church leaders, and laypersons are all involved in these historical projects, even if the results turn out in many cases to be constructed as an academic enterprise. This model argues that it is important to uncover the history of those who have been left out of the major narratives in order to engage in the construction of their identity and personhood, which have been suppressed or falsely constructed by those in power.

Organized by time periods and regions, this anthology contains a collection of articles that focus on introducing histories about the development of the Latina/o church in the United States, and even includes one article on Latina/o Protestantism, which I discuss in the next chapter. The histories offer new perspectives on voices previously covered, but as a whole the collection seems to be more about the institution, that being the Catholic Church, than about the people. While the Latina/o people are at the center of the material being uncovered, they appear to be objects, as they are mostly reacting to the attitudes and actions of the institution. In this way the project achieves its purpose of looking at history from a different perspective, but it is still primarily a history of the church.

Moises Sandoval followed *Fronteras* with *On the Move: A History of the Hispanic Church in the United States*.[6] Looking at it, one can see that this work is a short and integrated version of *Fronteras*. This work represents an initial attempt to put together a coherent historical narrative regarding the religious life of Latinas/os in the United States, especially as it relates to the growth of this community within

[4] Moises Sandoval, ed., *Fronteras: A History of the Latin American Church in the USA since 1523* (San Antonio, Tex.: Mexican American Cultural Center, 1983).

[5] Ricardo Ramirez, "Preface," in Sandoval, *Fronteras*, vii.

[6] Moises Sandoval, *On the Move: A History of the Hispanic Church in the United States* (Maryknoll, N.Y.: Orbis, 1990). The importance of this work is exemplified by the fact that it was published as a second edition in 2006.

the Catholic Church and the development of different ministries and programs within this institution. At the work's core we find the same theoretical model of CEHILA that we referenced above, including the emphasis on the institutional history of the church. As in *Fronteras*, this approach allows for the voices of U.S. Latinas/os to become prevalent in the narrative. But, by introducing the stories of a community struggling with paternalistic and racist attitudes of the institution and its leaders, there is a danger of these narratives becoming mere stories of victimhood and not, as mentioned before, histories of subjecthood and agency. Following the liberationist paradigm, these two works seem to be concerned with opening the field of Catholic history in order to open the door for the development of ministries to Latina/o communities.

In 1994 the Cushwa Center for the Study of American Catholicism at the University of Notre Dame published a three-volume series on the history of Hispanic Catholicism in the United States. Grounded on that same liberationist spirit and compelled by the growth and number of Latina/o Catholics in the United States, the authors explore the way the Catholic Church has struggled to develop its ministries to these communities and how their presence changes and challenges the face and culture of the church. The first volume in this series, *Mexican Americans and the Catholic Church, 1900–1965*, deals with the multiple experiences of Mexican Americans in the United States.[7] In the introduction, the editors Jay P. Dolan and Gilberto M. Hinojosa make it clear that the purpose of the book is related to the capacity of the church to respond to the challenges the Latina/o community confronts in society. They state that, "before the Church, as institution and as people, can respond to the current crisis and devise a strategy for the future, it needs to reflect upon the past and understand the Mexican-American faith communities, their pre-twentieth-century roots, and their more recent development."[8] The book addresses this past, not simply as a narrative of the people's participation within the church, but also of the people's religious experiences outside the institution.

[7] Jay P. Dolan and Gilberto M. Hinojosa, eds., *Mexican Americans and the Catholic Church, 1900–1965* (Notre Dame: University of Notre Dame Press, 1994).

[8] Jay P. Dolan and Gilberto M. Hinojosa, "Introduction," in Dolan and Hinojosa, *Mexican Americans*, 2.

The book is divided into three sections that focus on the Mexican American Catholic experience by regions: Texas and the Southwest, California, and Midwest. While a different author writes each section, in each there is a focus on the development of parishes, their ministries, and the role they play within the community. The Mexican American Catholic experience is explored through the interplay between the institution and the community, with the authors highlighting the importance of the spirituality of the people both within and outside the institution. Some other issues and themes that help guide the narratives are migrations, *mestizaje*, and Americanization. But, at the core, these narratives are concerned with proving the importance and integration of the Mexican American experience within the larger Catholic experience in the United States. The editors write:

> Despite its failings, the Church ministered to the Mexicans and the Mexican Americans with great dedication and sacrifice. In all of the periods under study many European and Anglo-American priests and men and women religious spent their lives working among el pueblo, sometimes making the sacraments and education more available than it had been in their Mexican homeland. After a century of assimilating various Mexican religious traditions into the Church's devotional worship, the official Church in its support of the Cursillo movement in the 1960s backed the involvement of lay people in the preaching of the gospel, thus further incorporating into its mission Mexican-American culture and spirituality.[9]

Following this argument, one can identify the institution, not the people, as the subject of the narratives as they ascribe the incorporation of the Mexican religious traditions to the institution.

The second volume of the series examines the history of Puerto Rican and Cuban Catholic communities.[10] This work includes two narratives, one on each community, which, as in the previous volume, focus on the ministries of the Catholic Church toward the Latina/o community. Even when the institution seemed negligent at times, the authors find that the leaders of the local parishes were

[9] Dolan and Hinojosa, "Introduction," 8.

[10] Jay P. Dolan and Jaime R. Vidal, eds., *Puerto Rican and Cuban Catholics in the U.S., 1900–1965* (Notre Dame: University of Notre Dame Press, 1994).

creating welcoming communities that allowed the people to find a home and construct their identity without losing their culture. Reading further into the narratives, it is easy to see that these leaders were involved in a process of re-establishment of models for parishes and thus this book seems like a handbook to show not only the historical perspectives but also the activities/models that have worked as a ministry so that others may follow. In this sense, the issue of identity construction and survival takes center stage within these narratives. In the case of Cuba, the feeling of exile and the leaders that came in exile are responsible for the creation of the community and the survival of their cultural identity.

Transnational perspectives are essential to understanding both of these communities, and culture, including the African element within the culture, plays an important role in the way they preserve their identity and challenge the institution. The preservation of identity is what these two communities share. As the editors of this collection argue:

> Both Cubans and Puerto Ricans, whether rightly or wrongly, tend to perceive themselves as being here "provisionally"—until the economy allows them to return home to Puerto Rico; until Castro's fall allows them to return home to Cuba—and therefore insist on holding on to their language and culture, and strive to build communities of their own, where these values will be preserved. Even as many individuals strike roots in America, the "exile" mentality is held on to for psychological reasons.[11]

Through the establishment of a community in the United States by holding onto their cultures, these communities offer a model to resist the process of cultural Americanization present not only within the religious arena but also within society. In this book, the authors argue that these communities are built because of the work between the local clergy and the laity. Thus, while still focusing on the institution's role, these narratives open the door to look at the agency of the people in their own process of identity construction.

The third volume of this series tries to move beyond the regional and national perspective that guided the first two volumes.[12] While

[11] Jay P. Dolan and Jaime R. Vidal, "Introduction," in Dolan and Vidal, *Puerto Rican and Cuban Catholics*, 4.

[12] Dolan and Figueroa Deck, eds., *Hispanic Catholic Culture in the U.S.*

"the first two volumes consist of studies that identify and use the best primary and secondary sources and focus on manageable, discreet topics or themes," this volume moves "to assemble the material in new ways."[13] This is an anthology of eleven articles and a conclusion, all of which deal with multiple aspects of the Latina/o Catholic experience, ranging from a quick look at the history after 1965 (at which the other two volumes stop) to social identity to leadership to liturgy to Latina/o youth and Latina Catholics, among others. The articles in this collection were written from different perspectives, which the editors hope results "in a clearer conceptualization of the issues and in more substantial critical insights than were possible even a decade ago."[14] These new ways consist of new lenses of analysis such as gender, for example, that open the door for a reinterpretation of the histories.

In 1995 Timothy M. Matovina published his dissertation, *Tejano Religion and Ethnicity: San Antonio, 1821–1860,* which uncovers the history of the construction of identity in San Antonio by Spanish-speaking Catholics.[15] It is clear that Matovina was influenced by the same historical traditions revealed in the previous works. He challenges traditional narratives of the Tejano experience that traditionally did not include the Latina/o presence by arguing the theories and lenses used to read these histories has failed in its analysis because of its narrowness and simplistic understandings. Matovina argues that the inclusion of the Latina/o perspective not only opens the narratives to new stories and data, but also transforms the way one understands the larger history of the Tejano experience. He argues,

> This perspective reveals that theories of unilateral assimilation are inadequate for understanding the Tejano experience. It also suggests that pluralism does not necessarily entail a dominant group at a society's center tolerating some degree of diversity on the periphery. Rather, pluralism can also result from various groups in the same society who have not reached a consensus on which group is dominant and normative.[16]

[13] Dolan and Figueroa Deck, "Introduction," 1.

[14] Dolan and Figueroa Deck, "Introduction," 1.

[15] Timothy M. Matovina, *Tejano Religion and Ethnicity: San Antonio, 1821–1860* (Austin: University of Texas Press, 1995).

[16] Matovina, *Tejano Religion,* ix–x.

In order to challenge the normative understanding of pluralism, Matovina follows an analysis of what some may call the "contact and exchange" between the different groups in San Antonio, especially as it pertains to religion.

Matovina finds that religion plays an important role in the construction of identity within this period; with this in mind, he examines primary sources and documents of the time in order to provide a larger context and narrative beyond the ones economic and political histories have provided in the past. His analysis "is augmented by pertinent secondary literature, including reference to works on religion and ethnicity in American life that enhance an assessment of the San Antonio Tejano experience from 1821 to 1860."[17] This historical narrative includes the voices of those primary documents but also includes an analysis of the way religious life and rituals play an important role in the construction of ethnic identity, which connects this work with previous works that have been guided by the question of religion and identity.

Following this same interest in the construction of identity, Thomas A. Tweed wrote *Our Lady of the Exile: Diasporic Religion at a Cuban Catholic Shrine in Miami*.[18] This is one of the first academic historical projects on U.S. Latina/o religions that involves a look at the way religious rituals play an important role not only in the construction of identity but in the history of the community. This type of work is closer to those within the "lived religion" school of analysis, which I discuss in detail in the third part of the book. It is based on uncovering experiences and rituals that help construct an identity, which in this sense is a diasporic identity.

Through ethnographic exploration as a participant observer and an analysis of historical documents and interviews, Tweed explores the history of Cubans in Miami and the way the symbol of Our Lady of Charity and its shrine offer an outlook to the development of this history. This was a new way of looking at history; he examines the connection between religious identities and national identities through analysis of the multiple meanings of symbols. Since the story of the shrine sheds light on the history of the community, Tweed engages in an exploration of material culture such as

[17] Matovina, *Tejano Religion*, 2.

[18] Thomas A. Tweed, *Our Lady of the Exile: Diasporic Religion at a Cuban Catholic Shrine in Miami* (New York: Oxford University Press, 1997).

rituals and spaces. He argues that "These textual sources highlighted beliefs, as most scholarship on religion in the United States has, yet I was convinced that artifacts also inscribe meanings. For this reason, I studied the community's material culture as well—architecture, yard shrines, photographs, paintings, key chains, holy cards, and plastic statues—for clues about how those express and shape attitudes about religion and place."[19] This look at material culture is specifically important to immigrant communities that are, as developed by previous works, trying to resist cultural assimilation. Thus, through the analysis of material culture (and its importance) Tweed expands on the way scholars have looked at the role religion plays in the organization of migrant communities as he proposes that "transnational religious narratives might be ordered by appealing to the subthemes of mapping, meeting, and migration."[20]

This interest in religious experiences and identity construction thus became the major lens through which most scholars constructed their historical narratives about Latina/o Catholicism in the United States. But still the lack of primary sources made the development of this field difficult. In *¡Presente!: U.S. Latino Catholics from Colonial Origins to the Present*, the editors put together a collection of primary documents that locate the history of U.S. Latina/o Catholic community and identity within the larger U.S. Catholic experience, and the collection clearly addresses the need for more primary sources.[21] The editors recognize that there is not one Latina/o Catholic experience but many, and for that matter, "This book explores the complex and multiple ways Hispanic Catholics have forged and expressed identities in the midst of these varied experiences that comprise the mosaic of U.S. Catholicism."[22] Hence, it does not homogenize history, as it understands the challenges that, for example, national identities have raised in the development of these communities.

Structurally, this book follows a chronological approach, but it is divided by themes. Each section has an introduction, which becomes a historical narrative on a period of time that delineates the important issues, specifically as they pertain to the construction of identity. After each introduction, there is a collection of primary

[19] Tweed, *Our Lady of the Exile*, 6.

[20] Tweed, *Our Lady of the Exile*, 137.

[21] Matovina and Poyo, *¡Presente!*

[22] Matovina and Poyo, "Introduction," xv–xvi.

documents from that era that demonstrate the themes explored in the section. These documents help build the field of Latina/o Catholic religious history by offering historical sources of analysis, which in this case focus on the role of religion in the construction of identities. But the editors want to locate this work within the larger field of Latina/o studies, which had not included religion as a major criterion of analysis. Thus, *¡Presente!* wants to be situated as "the first book-length work to address explicitly the role of religion in the formation of Latina and Latino identities."[23] Furthermore, the editors find that works within Latina/o studies "often explore Latino Catholics' effort to engage their faith as a resource for cultural survival and social change; they also frequently criticize Catholicism as institutionally negligent or as a mechanism of social control over Latinos."[24] But this work is different because it moves the field forward as it "provides primary documents and analysis of Latina and Latino Catholic identities that will enable colleagues in Latino studies to examine religion in greater depth and with a stronger grasp of its significance and complexity."[25]

Following on the issue of identity in *¡Presente!* and building upon his initial work *Tejano Religion and Ethnicity*, Timothy Matovina engages in a deeper look and analysis of the devotion to Our Lady of Guadalupe at the San Fernando Cathedral in San Antonio in his *Guadalupe and Her Faithful: Latino Catholics in San Antonio, from Colonial Origins to the Present.*[26] His examination of this devotion opens the door to understanding the experience of Latina/o Catholics in this city and thus this approach to the ritual is similar to the type of work Tweed did with his study of Our Lady of Charity in Miami. While the author does not intentionally situate this work within the lived religions approach, it is important to recognize that this book is part of the Lived Religions series. The importance of this fact is that it offers the reader a hint of the kind of analysis embedded within the narrative.

Matovina uses ethnographic observation as a participant within the rituals in order to achieve an analysis of the meanings of these

[23] Matovina and Poyo, "Introduction," xvi.

[24] Matovina and Poyo, "Introduction," xviii.

[25] Matovina and Poyo, "Introduction," xviii.

[26] Timothy Matovina, *Guadalupe and Her Faithful: Latino Catholics in San Antonio, from Colonial Origins to the Present* (Baltimore: Johns Hopkins University Press, 2005).

religious experiences and the way these experiences help in the "making" of a community and the construction of an identity. He examines the relationship between the institution and the people (clergy vs. laity) as the laity assumes some control over particular aspects of the devotion. Hence, he acknowledges that, "Though priests typically have the final authority in liturgical matters such as adornment of the church worship space, San Fernando congregants have influenced the clergy's choices by their level of participation in fundraising campaigns, as well as by choosing their own sacred images to donate."[27] Most of those engaged in these campaigns are women, and through their role within the devotion and the practices women have been able to challenge some of the perceptions of women as simple participants since "Guadalupe celebrations have often enabled women to exercise greater leadership and authority than they have been able to in other areas of public life, illustrating what Ana María Díaz-Stevens calls the 'matriarchal core' of Latin American Catholicism."[28] The presence of this analysis is important because it represents one of the first times that gender became part of the examination of the past and the writing of a narrative within this field.

For Matovina, the analysis of the history of this devotion and its rituals at San Fernando provides proof of multiple interrelationships between religious traditions and the members of the community since some people were moved by the devotion and others saw it with disdain. He writes, "Thus the history of San Fernando reveals a range of possibilities for individual and collective empowerment that religious traditions like Guadalupan devotion can mediate, gloss over, or restrict."[29] This follows the same argument Tweed makes about the importance of place and how its understanding sheds light on the social and cultural contexts and the multiple meanings of the rituals. In his assessment, Matovina is self-aware of his own social location and how this may impact his own reading, and that is why he is explicit about the core of his analysis as he states, "I foreground in my analysis the insights, convictions, sentiments, and ritual actions of San Fernando's Guadalupan devotees."[30] In the same way, he is also

[27] Matovina, *Guadalupe and Her Faithful*, 16.
[28] Matovina, *Guadalupe and Her Faithful*, 18.
[29] Matovina, *Guadalupe and Her Faithful*, 19.
[30] Matovina, *Guadalupe and Her Faithful*, 21.

clear about the purpose of the book by acknowledging that he wants "to increase appreciation and critical understanding of this fascinating faith expression and to help animate its ongoing celebration and development."[31] Despite what seems to be a simplistic primary purpose, that of promoting the devotion, I argue this work goes beyond that as it challenges the way one may look at the history of Latina/o Catholics in the United States. Through this approach to the study of ritual and space, scholars are able to open the historical discourses to the voices of practitioners and not just to the voices of the leaders. It is a way of doing history "from below," as the CEHILA framework promotes, by putting the voices of the people over the work of the institution.

In another work dealing with a particular city, Roberto R. Treviño examines the important role Catholicism has played in the development of the Mexican American community in Houston in his *The Church in the Barrio: Mexican American Ethno-Catholicism in Houston*.[32] Specifically, Treviño is interested in "*how* has that importance revealed itself in the Mexican American experience."[33] The urban setting is important in the construction of this narrative as a social history. While Tweed's and Matovina's works are also situated within cities, their focus on rituals and space situates the shrine and the cathedral, respectively, at the center of their discourses. For Treviño, the experiences of people in the barrio informs his analysis of the ways the Catholic Church has "related" to the people. In this sense, he is interested in the official experiences of the people within the church as much as their religious experiences outside the institution.

Furthermore, he argues that even differentiating between these experiences by attributing legitimacy to one and not the other is problematic. He argues:

> I do not rigidly juxtapose the institution's religion against the people's. Framing religious experience as dichotomies—"elite versus popular" or "folk versus formal" religion—may indeed reveal struggles between the powerful and the less powerful in

[31] Matovina, *Guadalupe and Her Faithful*, 21.

[32] Roberto R. Treviño, *The Church in the Barrio: Mexican American Ethno-Catholicism in Houston* (Chapel Hill: University of North Carolina Press, 2006).

[33] Treviño, *Church in the Barrio*, 4 (emphasis in original).

> a society, but it also distorts historical reality. Such neat categories simply do not convey the complexities of the *interaction* that has characterized the relationship between the faithful and religious institutions.[34]

Breaking away from this dichotomy, Treviño is able to locate his work outside a theological discourse and within a historical discourse.

Treviño's main interest is in Mexican American history and how a type of Catholicism, which he refers to as Mexican American ethno-Catholicism, helps in understanding this history. This work represents a look at religion beyond the official history of a church, as he is interested in the analysis of how religious experiences inform the construction of this Mexican American Catholic community in Houston. He writes, "I hope to show that by understanding ethno-Catholicism we can more fully understand the construction of ethnic identity, the formation of communities, the sources and processes of social change, the ways people find their place in a society, and some of the implications of gender relations—subjects that too often are studied without much attention given to the role of religion."[35] Treviño's perspective here is consistent with the critique regarding the absence of religion in the majority of the works within Latina/o history in the United States.

In an effort to go beyond the analysis of the religious experiences of one particular Latina/o group in one city, but still focus on identity, David Badillo examines a multiplicity of Latina/o experiences from different nationalities and different geographical locations.[36] For him, "To fully understand Latinos in the United States today, one must understand their unique, complex and ever-evolving relationship with the Catholic Church, the Catholic religion, and the various syncretisms born of Catholic interactions in the Americas."[37] In order to highlight the importance of this relationship in the construction of U.S. Latina/o identities, Badillo engages in a comparative examination "of the religious histories of the three primary Latino groups—Mexican Americans, Puerto Ricans, and Cubans (and, to a lesser extent, more recent migrants)—highlighting distinctive

[34] Treviño, *Church in the Barrio,* 5 (emphasis in original).

[35] Treviño, *Church in the Barrio,* 7.

[36] David A. Badillo, *Latinos and the New Immigrant Church* (Baltimore: Johns Hopkins University Press, 2006).

[37] Badillo, *Latinos,* xi.

characteristics of each," in order to illuminate "differences and similarities among peoples of Latin American origin and in Latino Catholicism in different cities and regions."[38] His larger analysis is based on the construction of transnational identities and the role of religion in this process.

The book is put together through a thematic discussion under the umbrella of immigration and the effects of the constant movements of Latinas/os throughout the Americas, especially in the United States. This narrative is Catholic at its core and it follows the same interest Treviño puts into the construction of identity within the urban setting. Badillo argues that within this setting Latino Catholicism should be understood as part of the daily experience of what it means to be a U.S. Latina/o. At the same time, the urban setting affects the way this religion is lived and while there are regional differences, there is still a strong connection between the construction of a community and the religious experiences of the people. Now, contrary to what others in the past seemed to be trying to do, Badillo is not interested in simply putting the story of Latina/o religion within the context of U.S. Catholicism, but he is interested in grounding this story as part of the history of larger Latina/o identity. He includes a whole chapter on the European past of Latinas/os because he wants to demonstrate that this religious history was not created by U.S. Catholicism but converges with it. Thus, he does not focus on the history of the institutional Catholic Church but on the experience of the people, even if it is outside the church, as is popular Catholicism.

After Badillo's pioneering work, the focus on particular communities and regions has continued as scholars keep concentrating their analyses in the religious experiences of particular groups. Gerald E. Poyo continues this approach with his examination of Cuban Catholics.[39] His *Cuban Catholics in the United States, 1960–1980* may be seen as a continuation of 1994's *Puerto Rican and Cuban Catholics in the U.S., 1900–1965*, only concentrating on the Cuban community. Poyo focuses on the effects of the Cuban Revolution and the way religion is experienced in the midst of exile. By highlighting the cultural aspects of Cuban Catholics, he is able to show the history

[38] Badillo, *Latinos*, xi.

[39] Gerald E. Poyo, *Cuban Catholics in the United States, 1960–1980: Exile and Integration* (Notre Dame: University of Notre Dame Press, 2007).

of the community and the way its identity is built, an exile identity. In this regard, Poyo is clear that, "While Catholics represent only a small slice of the Cuban exile story, they offer a microcosm through which to explore in some detail and understand many of the themes relevant to the exile experience generally."[40] This analysis is similar to Tweed's understanding of diasporic identity, but Poyo goes beyond the experiences at the shrine.

The book's narrative is concerned with the relationship between exile identity and Catholic identity and how they intersect each other. For example, the author finds that the community has an interest to connect with the work of the church, and as such the church becomes part of the community. It is a social history that includes a look at the Cuban Catholic experience and how this experience is an intrinsic aspect of the transnational history, the political struggle, and the cultural experiences of the Cuban community. Poyo argues that, "By tracing in some detail the historical trajectory of Catholic personalities and actors, revealing their ideas and aspirations, and analyzing the meaning of their actions, this book aims to further the goal of writing the history of Cubans as exiles while also exploring their place in the broader landscape of U.S. history during the 1960s and 1970s."[41]

Even with all of these works and hundreds of articles, Latina/o Catholic history has not been given full consideration by the larger field of Latina/o studies or Chicana/o studies, but Mario T. García would like that to change, and he shows how with his *Católicos*.[42] García was motivated by "the dearth of research in Chicano Catholic history," even when other areas have been fully explored.[43] Following a liberationist paradigm, García constructs a narrative through the lenses of resistance and affirmation. This narrative is made up of not just one but multiple stories that provide proof of the centrality of religion within the Chicano experience and especially as an aspect of daily life.

This is a cultural history that connects political and social movements with the religious experience. In this sense García

[40] Poyo, *Cuban Catholics*, 3.

[41] Poyo, *Cuban Catholics*, 7.

[42] Mario T. García, *Católicos: Resistance and Affirmation in Chicano Catholic History* (Austin: University of Texas Press, 2008).

[43] García, *Católicos*, 12.

explores the intersections of the Chicano culture and identity and the Catholic experience, making his work similar in this way to Poyo's analysis of the Cuban community. In the introduction, the author makes the case for locating his work as part of the development of a historical discourse that helps in understanding the community's identity and that highlights the importance of religion in the construction of such an identity. He acknowledges that while the field of Chicano history has failed to include religion, the field of Latina/o religious history has failed to grasp the Chicano movement. In this regard García states:

> Approaching these themes under the rubric of resistance and affirmation, my book will bring greater attention to the importance of Chicano Catholic history in a reevaluation not only of Chicano historiography but also of Chicano studies as a whole and of U.S. Catholic history and Catholic studies. One cannot fully understand Chicanos, or any ethnic group for that matter, without taking into consideration the significant role played by religion in shaping community. In turn, one cannot do justice to the history of U.S. Catholicism without integrating the history of Chicano/Latino Catholics.[44]

For García the community includes the priests, the religious workers, and the activists as they all work together, which reflects Poyo's recognition that the work of the leaders of the church and the work of the laity intersect.

PARADIGMS WITHIN LATINA/O CATHOLIC HISTORIOGRAPHY

The themes and topics in these works are representative of the major issues exposed by the literature within the field, including many articles and nonscholarly works that I have not included here. At the same time, a look at these major works allows us to examine the key theoretical and methodological approach to the study of Latina/o Catholicism in the United States. I am not implying that scholars use only one particular method or theoretical lens since I understand that most historians use multiple approaches in the way they construct their narratives. What I am arguing is that this examination provides us with details about the growth of the field regarding the

[44] García, *Católicos*, 26.

type of methods and theoretical approaches that scholars have been able to develop throughout time.

The historiographical analysis reveals that there has been a movement away from the traditional historical narrativizing of the early works that were based on secondary sources in order to use more primary sources and ethnographical analysis. In order to explain this development, I propose that we look at the progression of the field in three phases. I am artificially defining these phases, not because there are clear and specific breaks between the different projects, but because this classification allows us to identify some of the transformations in approaches. Furthermore, I recognize that the presence of a liberationist approach as an overarching paradigm ties all of these works together, so my attempt to separate them into phases has the purpose of examining the other methodological and theoretical approaches they established.

FIRST PHASE: ESTABLISHING A PRESENCE

I trace the first stage of the development of the field to the works by Moises Sandoval and the Notre Dame history of Hispanic Catholicism in the United States. During this stage the interest was to locate the history of the Latina/o community within the history of the Catholic Church in the United States. Many of these narratives are based on secondary sources, and they focus on exposing the presence of this community within the Catholic institution. These works come out of the interest of scholars and church leaders to provide a voice for the community and the need to create ministries that address the community's needs.

As mentioned before, the construction of these narratives is founded on a liberationist approach, born out of the development of liberation theology in Latin America. It is important to spend some lines illustrating the importance of this theological and social movement, which opened the door for a new generation of scholars who "opted for the prophetic questioning of institutions and for liberation struggles that began to generate a whole new radical literature in history, social sciences and theology."[45] In regard to religious history,

[45] Samuel Silva-Gotay, "A Scientific History of the Latino Church," in *Hidden Stories: Unveiling the History of the Latino Church*, ed. Daniel R. Rodríguez-Díaz and David Cortés-Fuentes (Decatur, Ga.: Asociación para la Educación Teológica Hispana, 1994), 41.

the new questioning generated "a new historiography that took into consideration factors of class as well as the history of exploitation in society and its various links to Christianity."[46] This approach challenged the traditional ways of doing history.

Within the traditional ways, "history is usually written by the victors and not by the losers" because in this case "history is recorded by those who had the upper hand, while the equally heroic story of those who lost out is overlooked."[47] Through the use of a liberationist approach, scholars and church leaders examine history through different lenses: the voices and stories of those who have been silenced by the traditional normative historical narratives. At the same time, this new historiography connects the new stories, or new readings of old stories, to their sociopolitical and economic realities. The work of CEHILA exemplifies this approach, and sociologist Samuel Silva-Gotay clearly explains these efforts:

> With their work, CEHILA authors have incorporated the analysis of social sciences to the analysis of society, and finally to the analysis of the relation between church and society. Through this methodology, they not only ensure the rigorous use of primary documentation, but also the analysis of the church as a part of the developmental period of society and of the general history of religion or of the country. Therefore, they avoid uprooting church history from the material and social life that nurtures it.[48]

This historiographical vision not only became the structure behind the writings within this first phase, but it has shaped the underlining liberationist scaffold of the entire field and its interest in thinking from "the underside of history."[49]

The works within this first phase follow this perspective of history from below, but still they should be read within the context of an institutional history. The new voices and stories examined are put together in the context of the work of the church and the

[46] Silva-Gotay, "Scientific History," 41.

[47] Ricardo Ramírez, "Foreword," in Sandoval, *On the Move: A History of the Hispanic Church in the United States*, vii.

[48] Silva-Gotay, "Scientific History," 45.

[49] For more information on this type of approach, see Linda Martin Alcoff and Eduardo Mendieta, eds., *Thinking from the Underside of History: Enrique Dussel's Philosophy of Liberation* (Lanham, Md.: Rowman & Littlefield, 2000).

responses of the Catholic leadership and its ministry to the Latina/o community. In many ways these narratives, even when constructed from a different perspective, reflect the positivist paradigm of having order and lineality. They do not seem to be breaking the official institutional narratives, but simply adding more information to those narratives. Of course, these additions challenge traditional understandings, but the core of the normative narratives is maintained. In this sense, the works in the first phase illustrate the beginnings of a field, where the interest mostly resides in the dis-covery of new voices and stories, the rereading of the established narratives. The third volume of the Notre Dame series becomes that initial effort to move the field beyond this first stage, as it incorporates not just new themes but also new theoretical lenses and analytical tools, such as gender and ritual. It is based on these new analytical approaches on which the field grew and developed new methodologies.

SECOND PHASE: SEARCH FOR IDENTITY

The second phase of the development of the field is characterized by an in-depth analysis of identity construction. This analysis is based on the way Latinas/os experience religion and how these religious experiences inform who they are. It represents a movement from the first phase, as scholars in this phase are more interested in looking at the agency of the people and not so much at the role of the institution. Most of the works are concerned with the way an examination of the religious experiences of the people allows for the understanding of their history. The works by Timothy M. Matovina and Thomas A. Tweed are representative of this phase.

Within this phase scholars begin to use ethnographical approaches in case studies to explore the history of the community and their identity. Both Tweed and Matovina use this type of approach as they look at the importance of rituals in the process of constructing the identity of the community. They consider culture as an intrinsic aspect of the way one lives out religion. This type of approach has put social and cultural history at the forefront of Latina/o Catholic history, privileging social science methodologies. This is the reason why these works could be identified as following the lived religion paradigm, in which the agency of the people is demonstrated by their role within religious experiences. It has opened the field of Latina/o Catholic history as the people have become the center of the narratives. While the history of the Catholic institution is present within the narratives, it does not determine the actual content or the way the narratives are constructed.

As in the first phase, I find that there is a work that, while within the same phase, helps to move the field further, and that is Matovina and Poyo's *¡Presente!* This book shares the same interest in the construction of identity as others within this phase but because it includes a collection of original documents in a chronological order, one is able to see beyond the secondary sources. I argue that these materials open the door for students and scholars alike to research the area even further because these offer a window to the different stages, regions, and processes within the Latina/o Catholic experience. At the same time, it is essential to highlight the interest of the editors of this collection to impact the larger field of Latina/o studies with the inclusion of the importance of religion as a criterion of analysis in understanding of Latina/o history and the construction of identities within these communities. This concern is going to move the field into its third phase.

THIRD PHASE: RELIGION AS THEORY

While keeping their focus on the examination of identity as a way to understand history, the works within the third phase incorporate religion as a theoretical piece of the analysis. This implies that religion is no longer just an aspect to analyze as part of the examination of Latina/o history and identity, but that religious experiences should be used as one the lenses through which history can be understood. The same ethnographical, social, and cultural methodologies are still used. But, the approach to religion is what differentiates the works in this phase from the previous phase.

The literature within this phase, such as the works by Treviño, Badillo, and García, highlights the importance of religious experiences beyond the official history of the church. Religion in these cases is intertwined with culture and social location (i.e., transnational perspectives, urban settings, political struggle, etc.). In this sense, for these scholars their analyses are not about studying the role of religion in the life of the community, but about understanding religious experiences and using them to examine the development of the community, even beyond the church experience. This perspective challenges the absence of religion within the literature in the field of Latina/o studies while also challenging the field of

Latina/o Catholic history to see beyond the church structure and experiences.

This phase represents the state of the field as I write these words. Scholars continue to explore rituals, specific groups, and religious experiences at particular locations that keep enhancing the development of the field. Ethnography and other participatory methodologies associated with the social sciences have become the dominant modes of analysis, while at the same time scholars are connecting religious experiences to other criteria of analysis such as migration movements (i.e., Badillo and Poyo), and social and political agendas (i.e., García). On the other hand, criteria such as gender and transnationalism, which I explore in detail in the third part of this book, while present within some of the examinations, have not been used as central principles in the development of these historical narratives.[50] The inclusion of more criteria and new theories of analysis would continue to build a more comprehensive field.

[50] It is important to acknowledge that gender has been used in the development of other works, including Lara Medina, *Las Hermanas: Chicana/Latina Religious-Political Activism in the U.S. Catholic Church* (Philadelphia: Temple University Press, 2004), which I will explore later. Here, I am arguing that the projects that deal with general aspects of this history, not specific gender issues, do not intrinsically include gender as one of the criteria used to understand the history of the community.

4 PROTESTANT HISTORIES

Yet, the Protestant faith has been part of Hispanic Christianity for well over a century in this country and in Latin America.

—David Maldonado Jr., "Protestantes: An Introduction," in *Protestantes/Protestants*, 9

Like the histories of Latina/o Catholics, the histories of Latina/o Protestants in the United States have been slowly dis-covered. In the past decade, we have seen an increase in the publication of works in this area, and even though these projects have been overlooked by many in the dominant academic world, scholars and nonscholars have not stopped dis-covering these histories.[1] One of the reasons for this neglect is the presence of the stereotype of Latinas/os as Catholics. As David Maldonado Jr. explains:

> Hispanic Protestants have long been overlooked or regarded as an insignificant exception to the U.S. Hispanic religious reality. Because of the central and influential role that the Roman Catholic Church played in the exploration and establishment of Spanish Catholic rule in the Americas, and in the formation of the mestizo cultures of Mexico and Latin America, Hispanic populations

[1] The large amount of material (essays, theses, dissertations) in the past decades comes from people both within and outside the academy. An example of the amount of available material is the bibliography in the history section of Paul Barton and David Maldonado Jr., eds., *Hispanic Christianity within Mainline Protestant Traditions: A Bibliography* (Decatur, Ga.: Asociación para la Educación Teológica Hispana, 1998).

> have long been associated with Roman Catholicism with regard to culture, religious identity, and faith. As a result, there arose a long-standing assumption that to be Hispanic was to be Catholic. Hispanics were assumed to be a monolithic religious community, Catholic from their birth as a people, and Catholic in all aspects of their lives.[2]

Since Protestantism has dominated the normative historical discourses of U.S. religion, this stereotype offered an excuse for the disregard of historical narratives about Latinas/os, which in many cases have been not only ignored but labeled as particular or ethnic. Hence, the development of Latina/o Protestantism defies these assumptions and stereotypes.

Latina/o Protestant histories question and challenge the themes and the geographical locus of the dominant discourses in U.S. religious histories. The challenge comes as U.S. religious histories have been mostly focused on the northeastern Puritan tradition or on the establishment of a black/white paradigm, leaving the experience of the Latina/o community outside the discourse. This explains, in part, why leaders and laypersons of the Latina/o church did most of the production of the early Latina/o religious historical materials from the margins of the dominant historical discourse. In fact, the actual history has been being made outside the places of power within the denominations and other religious groups. As Daisy Machado argues, "It is in this other place, this place 'outside the gate,' where the Latina/o church can be found and where her history has been made, continues to be made, and is currently being lived and told."[3]

Now, with the upsurge in research on Latina/o Protestant histories, we need to consider this, along with the field of Latina/o Catholic histories, as an emergent field. Built on the analysis of Protestant missionary activities, this field has been evaluating the growth of Latina/o Protestant communities and developing discourses that expose issues of paternalism and the Americanization agenda behind these activities. Still, there are many issues to explore, and establishing solid theories and methodologies of analysis would assist in the development of the field.

[2] Maldonado, "Protestantes," in *Protestantes/Protestants: Hispanic Christianity within Mainline Traditions*, ed. David Maldonado Jr. (Nashville: Abingdon, 1999), 9.

[3] Daisy Machado, "The Writing of Religious History in the United States: A Critical Assessment," in Barton and Maldonado, *Hispanic Christianity*, 84.

In this chapter I evaluate some of the literature in the field of Latina/o Protestant history that exemplifies the evolution of this field. As I have mentioned before, my interest lies beyond the topics of the different works, as I am concerned with the approaches these follow in order to construct their narratives. Here, I follow the same structure as in the previous chapter. In the first part, through a historiographical survey, I examine some of the most important works in the field not only by looking at the major themes, but by focusing mostly on the way the scholars explore these themes and the lenses of interpretation they use.[4] Following the historiographical survey, I explore the development of the field by highlighting the major theories and methodologies of analysis found in the survey and how they have helped in the evolution of the field. To conclude the chapter I have added a third section, in which I compare and contrast the aspects of this field with the ones I found regarding the field of Latina/o Catholic history in order to have a better sense of the larger field of Latina/o religious history.

HISTORIOGRAPHICAL SURVEY

In 1933 Reverend Pablo García Verduzco published his *Bosquejo Histórico del Metodismo Mexicano en Texas y la Frontera de México*.[5] This is a seminal work, not only in the history of Latina/o Methodism in Texas and the borderlands, but also in the process of developing the history of Latina/o Protestantism, especially in the Southwest. García Verduzco's account is primarily a review of the missionary activity within the Methodist church and the establishment of congregations. He explores biographies, memoirs, and the work of missionaries and other laity, both Euro-Americans and Mexicans, which, linked together, constitute a history that, as Juan Martínez acknowledges, tends to be vague and difficult to follow.[6]

[4] As I have mentioned before, I recognize the presence of many works that deal with Latina/o religious history and in this case Latina/o Protestantism, but I focus my attention on a number of works that I believe are representative of the evolution of the field. Hence, my analysis is subjective to my comprehension of the field.

[5] Pablo García Verduzco, *Bosquejo Histórico del Metodismo Mexicano en Texas y la Frontera de México* (Nashville: Cokesbury Press, 1933).

[6] Juan Francisco Martínez, "Origins and Development of Protestantism among Latinos in the Southwestern United States, 1836–1900" (Ph.D. diss., Fuller Theological Seminary, 1996), 449.

This project was developed on the basis of the life stories of the leaders of the church since the author acknowledges the lack of resources and documentation.[7]

More than three decades later, in 1964 Kyle Haselden published *Death of a Myth: New Locus for Spanish American Faith*, which opened the discussion about Protestantism among Latinas/os in the United States, not just in one region or one denomination.[8] Haselden wants to prove that, "The assumption that all Spanish Americans are Roman Catholics and that Protestantism and Spanish American culture and personality are incompatible is a myth that must be repudiated in the Spanish American but particularly in the Anglo-American mind."[9] This work, mostly aimed at a white Euro-American audience, includes an examination of the diversity of people and groups that form the Latina/o community and their participation within Protestantism, especially as it pertains to the development of a Latina/o Protestant spirituality. For Haselden this spirituality could "redeem" white Protestant churches in the United States, which he finds "need a new stock to free them from their middle-class prison," and "from the stifling genteel mentality and the prim and proper morality of an affluent, status-seeking culture."[10] The presence of Latina/o Protestants changes the face of Protestantism and challenges the normative understandings of this religious culture.

At the same time, Haselden argues that this newfound spirituality helps Latinas/os "escape" from what he sees as the immorality of Catholicism. In effect, his critique of Catholicism is even harsher than the one he offers about Euro-American Protestantism, as he asserts:

> Finally, we see in the evangelical piety of Spanish American Protestants a revulsion against the immoralities tolerated by the Roman Catholic Church wherever it has been captured in Central and South American countries by the paganism and politics of those countries. The moral laxity and indifference of nominal Roman Catholics in Latin American countries is repudiated by the earnest evangelical Spanish American. Turning away from that moral

[7] García Verduzco, *Bosquejo Histórico*, 5–6.

[8] Kyle Haselden, *Death of a Myth: New Locus for Spanish American Faith* (New York: Friendship Press, 1964).

[9] Haselden, *Death of a Myth*, 12.

[10] Haselden, *Death of a Myth*, 155.

> laxity and indifference, the Spanish American seeks in embracing Protestantism a piety that not only renounces that kind of Catholicism but that satisfies his spiritual necessity.[11]

Thus, while critiquing Euro-American Protestantism on the one hand, Haselden perpetuates the nativistic ideology embedded within the missionary activities of the different Protestant groups on the other. This is critical in order to understand the value of this work. In addition to its examination of the presence of Latinas/os within Protestantism, the importance of this book lies in the exposition of this nativistic ideology, as it allows scholars to see beyond the mere missionary events and understand what lies behind them.

In 1974 Clifton L. Holland published *The Religious Dimension in Hispanic Los Angeles: A Protestant Case Study*, which provides an overview and analysis of the effects of Protestantism among Latinas/os in Los Angeles.[12] This is the first effort to compare and contrast the work of different Protestant denominations, including Pentecostal denominations, toward the Latina/o community, albeit in a particular setting.[13] At the center of this study of the growth of the Latina/o Protestant community in Los Angeles is not only the understanding of "the historical growth characteristics of the Spanish-speaking churches in the milieu of Southern California and Los Angeles county," but also ideas on how this understanding can provide "solutions to complex socioeconomic and ecclesiastical problems."[14] Through the use of historical and sociological perspectives, Holland is able to include detailed data regarding the number of Latino churches and their growth in membership, which results in a descriptive narrative of events.

That same year, R. Douglas Brackenridge and Francisco O. García-Treto first published *Iglesia Presbiteriana: A History of Presbyterians and Mexican Americans in the Southwest*.[15] The aim of the

[11] Haselden, *Death of a Myth*, 170–71.

[12] Clifton L. Holland, *The Religious Dimension in Hispanic Los Angeles: A Protestant Case Study* (South Pasadena, Calif.: William Carey Library, 1974).

[13] The inclusion of Pentecostalism is vital because not until the last decade have we had historical works on Latina/o Pentecostalism in the United States.

[14] Holland, *Religious Dimension*, xxxi.

[15] R. Douglas Brackenridge and Francisco García-Treto, *Iglesia Presbiteriana: A History of Presbyterians and Mexican Americans in the Southwest* (San Antonio, Tex.: Trinity University Press, 1987).

book is not only to trace the development of the missionary work of the Presbyterians to the Mexican Americans in the Southwest but also to construct a coherent historical account of this development. One of the first things the authors mention is the difficulty of their task since there is "a paucity of written material from Mexican American pastors and communicants."[16] Therefore, the official documents of the Presbyterian denominations became the major and sometimes only focus of study and scrutiny, and these documents were already infused with institutional bias. This book is thus part of an institutional (denominational) history and is clearly not developed from the perspective of the people.

These authors focused mainly on a chronology of events through which they wanted to expose the paternalistic attitudes of Euro-Americans towards Mexicans and Mexican Americans. They highlighted the lives of the leaders and missionaries of the church and their close relationships to the denomination. While the reading of the missionaries' attitudes constitutes an important aspect of retelling history, there is a lack of attention to the stories of the common people and an absence of consistent interpretation of the context and the characteristics of the people taking part in the life of the congregations. Only a few paragraphs at the beginning of each chapter are dedicated to this kind of interpretation. In this sense, this work follows the structure of a missionary history, within the context of a denomination (institution), in which the role of the missionary takes center place and the "recipients" of the message (the people) are seen as objects and not subjects of their own history. Hence, agency is still not present within this narrative.

This type of missionary approach is the same one that Joshua Grivalja follows in his *A History of Mexican Baptists in Texas, 1881–1981*, published 1982.[17] Grivalja wrote the history of a denomination within a particular space (Texas) and a particular group (Mexicans). This project focused on the dates, events, and figures that tell the story of the development of Baptist churches among Mexicans and Mexican Americans in Texas. It is mostly a study of the missionary enterprise and the later development of churches in this region from the perspective of the denomination. At the same time, as in the

[16] Brackenridge and García-Treto, *Iglesia Presbiteriana*, xiii.

[17] Joshua Grivalja, *A History of Mexican Baptists in Texas, 1881–1981* (Dallas: Baptist General Convention of Texas, 1982).

case of Brackenridge and García-Treto's work, this book illustrates some of the characteristics of the missionary enterprise such as the presence of paternalism and the control of the churches by the Euro-American leaders even with the growth of some native leadership. These observations are part of the presentation of the data within the book, but they exist without any interpretation. Thus, Grivalja's project should be identified as a historical chronology of a missionary activity lacking a strong interpretative framework.

In 1983 Randi Jones Walker finished her dissertation "Protestantism in Sangre de Cristos," which was later published as a book.[18] In this work, Walker explores the development of the Protestant missionary activity in the border area between New Mexico and Colorado, known as the Sangre de Cristo Mountains. The core of the narrative focuses on the interaction between the Euro-American Protestant culture and the Latina/o culture in this region, not by signaling to the dominance of one over the other, but by emphasizing the way they affect each other. This hermeneutical approach, which I refer to as contact and exchange, allows Walker to offer an analysis of the relationship between the two groups, missionaries and Latina/o community, in which the people are subjects and actors in the missionary activity, not merely beneficiaries (objects) of it as in the traditional missionary histories. Still, the missionary work is at the center of the narrative but the inclusion of the voice of the people adds a new perspective. It also opens the door to allow us to look beyond the work of the missionaries and the institution they represent and examine the rationale behind these activities.

Through an examination of local small newspapers and the writings of the local people, Walker is able to analyze the different attitudes of the missionaries and the people, especially as these different cultures collide. She finds that because these cultures are rooted in the same Western European civilization, and religion is central in each ethos, missionaries thought their work would not seem so abrupt, but that was not the result of this contact and exchange.

For example, Walker pays close attention to curriculum because she argues that education was vital in the development of the missionary work. She exposes these educational practices as instruments of the process of Americanization that the missionaries tried

[18] Randi Jones Walker, *Protestantism in the Sangre de Cristos, 1850–1920* (Albuquerque: University of New Mexico Press, 1991).

to impose upon the people. But, even with the cultural similarities and these educational practices, she argues that "Protestant impact on Hispanic Catholic culture in the Sangre de Cristos was minimal; only a small number of New Mexicans became Protestant."[19] This is one of the most important points Walker makes because it "illustrates the breaking point in the westward movement of American denominations."[20] She goes further to argue that, "In the Hispanic Catholic Southwest, Anglo-Americans encountered a culture which could neither be assimilated nor eradicated and thus challenged the foundational assumptions of a westward movement."[21] Here, the history of Protestantism among Latinas/os is connected to the larger story of the United States and not as a simple postscript of the official history, and that is one of the most important contributions of this work as it tries to break away from the traditional missionary narratives.

Also in 1983, Edwin Sylvest Jr. introduced an interpretative framework through which the development of Latina/o Protestantism should be analyzed. In his "Hispanic American Protestantism in the United States," an article in Moises Sandoval's *Fronteras: A History of the Latin American Church in the USA since 1513*, Sylvest introduces the U.S. Latina/o Protestant as a subject, not merely as the recipient of a missionary enterprise.[22] His thesis is that the development of Latina/o Protestantism can be explained "as a movement from oppression and dependence toward liberation and self-determination."[23] Hence, Sylvest argues in favor of the liberationist paradigm that characterized the Latina/o Catholic histories, as exposed in the previous chapter.

Unlike the other works I examine, this is a shorter piece that includes some general information, but not so much detail on events as the others. Still, this author puts the chronology of events in the context of the presence of Manifest Destiny and nativism. These become the interpretative lenses through which the events are

[19] Walker, *Protestantism*, 111.

[20] Walker, *Protestantism*, 118.

[21] Walker, *Protestantism*, 293.

[22] Edwin Sylvest Jr., "Hispanic American Protestantism in the United States," in *Fronteras: A History of the Latin American Church in the USA since 1513*, ed. Moises Sandoval (San Antonio, Tex.: Mexican American Cultural Center, 1983), 279–338.

[23] Sylvest, "Hispanic American Protestantism," 280.

interpreted. For Sylvest, these are defining ideological factors in the contact between Euro-American Protestantism and Mexicans and Mexican Americans in the Southwest, which is a similar to Walker's contact and exchange approach. Through his chronology of events, he is not interested in limiting his scope to a simple recounting of incidents, as was the case with Grivalja. Sylvest constructs a narrative filled with critical interpretations of the events that solidified his argument of liberation and self-determination. For example, instead of focusing on missionary activity, he focuses on the actions of the people and how their work provided the establishment of an indigenous base. These communities built independent judicatory organizations. For Sylvest these activities are what actually help explain the growth of Latina/o Protestantism, especially among Mexicans and Mexican Americans. This essay is important not only for the information it provides, but mostly because it becomes an example of how to incorporate interpretation (liberationist paradigm) within the narrative itself, and thus history is written from below.

In 1994 an anthology dealing with Latina/o Protestantism surfaced. *Hidden Stories: Unveiling the History of the Latino Church*, edited by Daniel R. Rodríguez-Díaz and David Cortés-Fuentes, is a collection of essays that covers a wide range of topics within Latina/o Protestantism, including methodological aspects.[24] This project is the result of the 1993 conference held at McCormick Theological Seminary on Latina/o Protestant church history.[25] The development of Latina/o theologies, biblical interpretations from a Latina/o perspective, and Latina women's experiences are among the themes explored, but it is the first section of the anthology that includes articles that deal with the methodological concerns about the study of Latina/o Protestant histories. Even when the articles offer multiple proposals about the direction of the field, these proposals follow

[24] Daniel R. Rodríguez-Díaz and David Cortés-Fuentes, eds., *Hidden Stories: Unveiling the History of the Latino Church* (Decatur, Ga.: Asociación para la Educación Teológica Hispana, 1994).

[25] This conference and this publication also gave way to the creation of an Academy for the Study of Latino Church History (APHILA), which was interested in developing projects around the study of Latina/o Protestantism in the United States. This organization did not last, and the actual momentum that may have been created with this publication was lost. The CEHILA USA group has come to fill some of that void, even if this group is ecumenical and does not only focus on Protestantism.

a liberationist paradigm in which it is a history done from the perspective of the oppressed.

These methodological discussions in *Hidden Stories* become the first attempt by scholars in the field to reflect about the status of the scholarship and research in the field and the possible approaches that could improve it, and to offer some direction. At the same time, these discussions take a their arguments step further, offering critiques of the dominant U.S. religious historical discourses for silencing marginal voices. These methodological proposals are built upon the importance of culture and identity as lenses of analysis that not only allow for the reinterpretation of the historical data, but also for the challenge of the way this data has been narrativized by the dominant discourses. For the scholars in this collection, breaking down normative knowledge begins with situating the study of the history of the Latina/o Protestant church with the people that make that history, in the borderlands of society, not with the discourses that identify those people as Others. In many cases, this anthology becomes the basis for the revitalization of the field by looking at Latina/o Protestant histories from a nonmissionary perspective and developing lenses of interpretation that highlight the agency of the community. This perspective is the one future publications built upon.

In the late 1990s, three other scholars finished their dissertations about Latina/o Protestantism in the United States, and all three were published in the next decade. These continued to focus on the Southwest and the Mexican and Mexican American communities Juan Francisco Martínez in his *Sea la Luz: The Making of Mexican Protestantism in the American Southwest, 1829–1900* traces the history of the origins, development, and later decline of Protestantism among Latinas/os in the Southwest in the nineteenth century.[26] Martínez focuses on the missionary activities of different Protestant denominations and finds that the first decades of work by Euro-American Protestants in this region were not successful, as "the Mexican American community did not readily accept Protestantism, and there were very few converts during the early years."[27]

[26] Juan Francisco Martínez, *Sea la Luz: The Making of Mexican Protestantism in the American Southwest, 1829–1900* (Denton: University of North Texas Press, 2006).

[27] Martínez, *Sea la Luz*, 3.

These findings are similar to Walker's argument on the development of Protestantism in the Sangre de Cristos, and Martínez' approach is also similar to that of Walker.

Sea la Luz incorporates a look at the work of the missionaries and their attitudes and motives with an analysis of the life of the early Mexican Protestants in order to understand the actual impact of the missionary enterprise. Martínez takes a closer look at the role of this enterprise in the process of assimilation but concludes that Mexicans, after converting to Protestantism, were able to construct an identity independent from the Euro-American Protestant culture. The missionaries, on the other hand, were confronted with a predicament because "most U.S. Protestants did not want Mexican Americans to continue as Catholics, but neither were they willing to accept them as equals when they became Protestants."[28] This contact and exchange between missionaries and people is at the core of Martínez' argument, but unlike Walker's work this relationship is explored beyond the cultural interaction as Martínez considers the process of identity construction. In the same way, it is important to allude to the presence of vast bibliographical material, statistics, and data, organized in tables and diagrams, as these represent valuable and significant resources in the field. *Sea la Luz* represents more movement away from a traditional missions history approach, even if most of the material comes from missionary documents, as the people take a more active role in the narrative.

Daisy L. Machado in her *Of Borders and Margins: Hispanic Disciples in Texas, 1888–1945* also continues to move the field forward as she examines the development of the disciples' missions to Latinas/os in Texas.[29] As scholars before, she uses the institution's official data for her analysis, but Machado understands both the importance of not simply identifying the events and the people involved in this history and the importance of analyzing the ethos in which this history took place. She finds that this ethos, this location, would explain the characteristics of the origins and development of this mission. To be able to examine the ethos, and for that matter the data, Machado uses the concept and ideology of frontier as the hermeneutical key. On the one hand, the frontier means a borderland for Latinas/os in

[28] Martínez, *Sea la Luz*, 145.

[29] Daisy Machado, *Of Borders and Margins: Hispanic Disciples in Texas, 1888–1945* (New York: Oxford University Press, 2003).

Texas, a place where people struggle and survive, and on the other hand, the frontier is the ideology of progress, movement, and conquering that not only helped in the development of the Christian church (Disciples of Christ) identity but also in building the identity of the nation.

Of Borders and Margins tackles the larger dominant historical discourse in the United States by challenging Frederick Jackson Turner's frontier thesis and the way this idea has misinformed the reading of the religious historical discourses of Texas. In explaining what the absence of critical perspectives creates, Machado argues that one misses the complexities of the Texas borderlands. She states:

> By uncritically preserving these interpretative lenses in our own historical discourse what has been lost is the importance of the people who lived in and shaped the borderlands. Lost is the crucial examination and recognition of the vitality of the borderlands itself as a place in which a *new* culture was shaped. By assuming that the Texas borderlands was a forgotten land, or that the borderlands was a place where the "superior" displaced "inferior," the deeper levels of meaning that belong to borderlands history is neglected. The complexities of life in the Texas borderlands remain unexamined.[30]

Machado dismantles these obsolete lenses in order to uncover the ideology behind the missionary activities. Once the historiographical discourse is scrutinized, the writing of history will consciously challenge—or promote—the dominant discourse. In this work, she challenges the discourse by arguing for a history beyond the "wilderness" myth so embedded in the national self-understanding.[31]

The ideology of the frontier thesis has been used to understand and construct the historical narratives about the westward movement of the pioneers while at the same time it has guided the missionary activities of Euro-Protestants. In the case of disciples, Machado finds that "instead of reshaping or molding the frontier ideals of land, Manifest Destiny, chosen people, to 'the genius of Christianity,' the Disciples uncritically incorporated these into their missions theology."[32] She is aware that this is not a matter of simply

[30] Machado, *Of Borders and Margins*, 18 (emphasis in original).

[31] Machado, *Of Borders and Margins*, 18–19.

[32] Machado, *Of Borders and Margins*, 105.

narrating a one-sided story, but that it is important to interpret the events, data, and ideology behind the story. The fact that Machado exposes that the principles behind the dominant historical discourse are connected to the ideology behind the missionary activity demonstrates the importance of acknowledging the discourse in the field before writing any kind of history. It is a way of understanding the Latina/o Protestant histories in the larger context.

The third manuscript, Paul Barton's *Hispanic Methodists, Presbyterians, and Baptists in Texas,* also highlights the contact and exchange between missionaries and the community.[33] As in the case of Martínez and Machado, Barton examines the way the Protestant missionary enterprise did or did not facilitate the assimilation of the Mexican American community. He also finds that grasping the effect of conversion in the process of assimilation is complicated. He explains, "The development of an emerging indigenous Mexican-American Protestant group calls into question the idea that Mexican Americans simply assimilated into mainstream American society through their participation in the Protestant church."[34] Mexican American Protestants developed their own type of Protestantism, which has allowed them to maintain their cultural identities while also providing them with some connections to the dominant society.

Barton uses identity construction (identity integration) to prove that Latina/o Protestantism does not fit one simple category, but is multifaceted. By examining both worlds and the interplay between Mexican American culture (including the Catholic background) and the Euro-American Protestant culture (including the anti-Catholicism embedded within), he provides evidence of the complexity of Mexican American Protestant identities. While it is not used within Barton's work, the concept of "in-betweenness," which I explore later in this book, comes to mind in this community struggle between keeping a cultural identity and fitting into the world of the dominant culture.

The examination of the Mexican American Protestant culture includes a look at conversions, music, and other aspects of their worship. Through their religious practices this community was able to

[33] Paul Barton, *Hispanic Methodists, Presbyterians, and Baptists in Texas* (Austin: University of Texas Press, 2006).

[34] Barton, *Hispanic Methodists,* 5.

put the two worlds together as exemplified in the case of the singing of *coritos* (short hymns). Barton states:

> Coritos assisted Latino/a Protestants in the formation of their religious and cultural identity in the midst of an often alienating society. They provided a theological reflection upon the concrete struggles of los Protestantes and placed Hispanic Protestants' life situation in the context of their relationship with the divine. Coritos are an example of the dialogical consciousness of Mexican-American Protestants, the inner and outer dialogue that occurs among Mexican Americans as they live in an Anglo-American society.[35]

This methodological turn in the analysis of the missionary enterprise locates the people at the center, not the missionaries, as they are active participants in their history and not passive recipients of missionary activity. Hence, *Hispanic Methodists, Presbyterians, and Baptists in Texas* follows the trajectory of moving away from traditional methodologies of missionary histories. While Barton compares his own approach to that of Holland and Walker, as both "compare and contrast the development of Latino/a Protestant traditions in a specific region,"[36] I argue that the approach Barton uses is different because it includes discussions and evaluations of the actual experiences of the people and does not follow a simple descriptive approach, which I argue is the one the other two follow.

In 1999 *Protestantes/Protestants: Hispanic Christianity within Mainline Traditions*, edited by David Maldonado Jr., was published and opened the studies of Latina/o Protestantism to multiple perspectives.[37] This work, as an anthology, is important not simply because of the historical articles in the first section, but because the totality of the collection situates Latina/o Protestants within the larger Latina/o culture, challenging the common understandings of that culture being intrinsically Catholic. *Protestantes/Protestants* locates Latina/o Protestant culture and ministry in the margins of the larger society and even the margins the Latina/o community. Thus, as I mentioned reviewing Barton's work, members of this

[35] Barton, *Hispanic Methodists*, 98.

[36] Barton, *Hispanic Methodists*, 8.

[37] Maldonado Jr., *Protestantes/Protestants*.

group find themselves in an "in-between" space from which they construct an identity. While not focusing so much on methodologies and theories of analysis, this collection follows in the tradition of *Hidden Stories* as it tries to promote not just consciousness about the development of Latina/o Protestantism but also future research in this field.

This book includes articles from historical, theological, sociological, and ministerial perspectives, and it is this diversity of approaches that allows scholars in the field of Latina/o Protestant history to recognize the possibility of other methodologies and theories beyond the analysis of the missionary enterprise. In the majority of the articles, Latina/o Protestants take center stage and are the subjects of their own story, not recipients or passive participants. The people are seen as agents of their own transformation and identity construction. These perspectives are revealed through approaches such as lived religion, ritual studies, and racial/ethnic analysis, among others. Hence, as I explore in the next section, these are approaches to build upon in order to keep examining the religious history of Latinas/os in the United States.

Except for Clifton L. Holland's *The Religious Dimension in Hispanic Los Angeles*, much of the research was concerned with mainline Protestant traditions, overlooking the histories of the Latina/o Pentecostal traditions, until the publication of *Latino Pentecostal Identity: Evangelical Faith, Self, and Society* in 2003.[38] Arlene M. Sánchez Walsh from the beginning of this work is clear about the purpose and the approaches she uses in the book; as she writes,

> This book examines the interplay between religious and ethnic identity among Latino Pentecostals/charismatics for clues to how they negotiate their varied identities. The Assemblies of God, Victory Outreach, and the Vineyard are studied to determine how they have created their religious identity and that identity has intermingled with their ethnic identity. Through fieldwork, oral histories, and surveys, this project found that Latino Pentecostals/charismatics have an ambivalent relationship with their ethnic identity.

[38] Arlene M. Sánchez Walsh, *Latino Pentecostal Identity: Evangelical Faith, Self, and Society* (New York: Columbia University Press, 2003).

For Sánchez Walsh, the process of identity construction reveals the histories of Latina/o Pentecostals. These histories challenge Latina/o histories and mainstream Evangelical histories, as Latina/o Pentecostals prove not to fit either of the traditional ways these are seen and constructed. This work provides evidence that Latina/o Pentecostals have constructed not only their own identity but also their own subculture, not dependent upon the white Pentecostal tradition or simply responding to the Latina/o Catholic culture.

The fact that she explores the experiences of the people through ethnographic work allows Sánchez Walsh to see beyond traditional understandings and brings her closer to the actual perspective of the participants. To do this is to open the narrative to the agency of the people because, as I mentioned above, Latina/o Protestants, Pentecostals in this case, are the actors of their history and the constructers of their identity. At the same time, Sánchez Walsh is able to offer her analysis on her findings using multiple lenses of interpretation like race, gender, and class in order to read the multiple relationships between the people and the leaders. Thus, this work is not only groundbreaking as "it represents one of the first academic historical narrative work about Pentecostals, specifically Mexican American Pentecostals, but also introduces new methodologies from the social sciences to the field of historical studies.[39]

In 2004 Juan F. Martínez Guerra and Luis Scott published the anthology *Iglesias Peregrinas en Busca de Identidad: Cuadros del Protestantismo Latino en los Estados Unidos*.[40] This collection includes articles dealing with multiple Latina/o Protestant histories (e.g., American Baptists, Assemblies of God, Apostolic Assembly of the Faith on Christ Jesus), and different themes (e.g., acculturation, hymnology, use of mass media) that facilitate the process of

[39] It is important to acknowledge that while I argue that this book is the first historical narrative on Pentecostalism among Latinas/os in the United States, specifically Mexican Americans, there have been other works on different aspects of Latina/o Pentecostalism that include historical data. See Eldin Villafañe, *The Liberating Spirit: Toward an Hispanic American Pentecostal Social Ethic* (Grand Rapids: Eerdmans, 1993).

[40] Juan F. Martínez Guerra and Luis Scott, eds., *Iglesias Peregrinas en Busca de Identidad: Cuadros del Protestantismo Latino en los Estados Unidos* (Buenos Aires: Ediciones Kairós, 2004). This book has been translated and is now available in English; see Juan F. Martínez Guerra and Luis Scott, eds., *Los Evangélicos: Portraits of Latino Protestantism in the United States* (Eugene, Ore.: Wipf & Stock, 2009).

understanding the construction of Latina/o Protestant identity. The diversity of Protestant denominations explored, mainline and Pentecostal alike, make this work unique as it expands the discourse of Latina/o Protestantism that, as evidenced from its absence in many previous works, has not included Pentecostalism as part of the community. It is as a CEHILA project, and at the core of the arguments in the different articles one finds the liberationist paradigm. Like *Hidden Stories* and *Protestantes/Protestants*, this collection, with a multiplicity of themes and approaches, keeps moving the field away from traditionally missionary perspectives to new theoretical and methodological perspectives that focus on the present actions of the community and how that helps in the understanding of Latina/o Protestant history.

A year later, Rudy V. Busto published his *King Tiger: The Religious Vision of Reies López Tijerina*, which connects the field of Latina/o Protestant history with the larger field of Chicano studies.[41] This work focuses on examining the life of the great Chicano leader Reies López Tijerina, not in terms of his political involvement but in terms of the religious impetus behind his actions. Busto argues that while many have written on the life of Tijerina, in order to fully understand his life as a Chicano leader it is important to analyze his religious vision(s). This is not only as rereading of Tijerina's work but also a reinterpretation of the normative discourse about his life within the canon of Chicana/o studies.

King Tiger, at its core, is a conversation between religious studies and ethnic studies in order to grasp the importance of religion for minority groups in their struggle for justice. But, at the same time, Busto finds that both fields have forgotten about Tijerina and the important role religion played in his life. He situates Tijerina's religious vision within the context of the Southwestern experience, which exemplifies the importance of always contextualizing our histories so that we do not fall prey to the positivist understanding of knowledge as absolute. His approach of rereading and reinterpreting the narratives of the past, with the inclusion of new interviews and data, serves as an example of the present possibilities of dis-covering the stories of the past in order to offer new perspectives on Latina/o Protestant history and challenge the traditional discourses.

[41] Rudy V. Busto, *King Tiger: The Religious Vision of Reies López Tijerina* (Albuquerque: University of New Mexico Press, 2005).

PARADIGMS WITHIN LATINA/O PROTESTANT HISTORIOGRAPHY

The previous historiographical analysis provides us with a better look at the major themes and theoretical perspectives present within the field. For example, it is obvious that much of the literature has focused on particular denominations, making some of the discourses close to institutional histories.[42] In the same way, the Southwest and Mexican American Protestant culture has become the core social location of these studies. But, even with these aspects dominating the larger extent of the literature, we can see the development of the field not simply in terms of the data and themes dis-covered, but also in the approaches used.

Latina/o Protestant history, as an emergent field, has gone through changes as more scholars have gotten involved and brought different perspectives to these studies. The most important change is the development of the field from a missionary history approach to a cultural and social history of the community from the perspective of the people. The incorporation of a liberationist paradigm helped in this development as it opened the field to the "underside" of history, to look at the past in light of the experience of the oppressed. Still, it is this perspective that guides much of the research in the area in the present day.

As I did in the previous chapter, I propose to look at this development in phases, even if they are artificially defined since there are no clear breaks in the progress of the field that make these divisions apparent. This exercise, which in this case seems harder than in the previous chapter, allows us to scrutinize better the movement and progression of the field from one approach to another, even as scholars use multiple approaches. I argue for the existence of three major phases.

[42] Among other denominational histories that I did not examine here are Alfredo Náñez, *History of the Río Grande Conference of The United Methodist Church* (Dallas: Bridwell Library-Southern Methodist University, 1980); and Justo González, ed., *En Nuestra Propia Lengua: Una Historia del Metodismo Unido Hispano* (Nashville: Abingdon, 1991). While the former deals with one conference of the United Methodist Church, each chapter of the latter is dedicated to the history of United Methodism among Latinas/os in a particular region of the United States.

FIRST PHASE: CHRONICLES OF A MISSIONARY ACTIVITY

This phase is characterized for its descriptive approach to the missionary activities, and in the case of Holland, a descriptive approach of the ministries toward Latinas/os in a particular urban setting. Authors like García Verduzco, Brackenridge and García-Treto, and Grivalja were interested in describing the activities of the Protestant missionaries to Latinas/os, specifically the Mexican American community. While there is some examination of the paternalistic attitudes embedded within the missionary enterprise, these works do not contain in-depth analysis of these activities. The main characters of these narratives are the missionaries and some of the leaders of the community, but members of the community at large become passive participants, recipients of the message. Because of the connection of most of these narratives to institutional histories, the authors engaged in highlighting the ministries created by the church to the Latina/o community in order to emphasize the importance of this community in the life of the church. In this phase, at the core of the narratives one finds a chronology of events and a dissemination of data in which the leaders, those in power, are the protagonists of the action. The missionary activity and ministerial work are described but not examined from the perspective of the people.

SECOND PHASE: LIBERATIONIST PARADIGM

The second phase of the development of the field is characterized by the process of scrutiny of missionary activity and the ideology behind it, and the establishment of a historical voice of the people as active participants in the narratives. The work of Randi Walker Jones should be located within the first and the second phase because while it does not include a strong methodological approach that opens the door to the voices of the people, it does contain an evaluation of the ideology behind the missionaries' work. This type of analysis was also present in Haselden's work, but still from the perspective of those in power, not necessarily from the perspective of the Latina/o community.

Through the use of the liberationist paradigm, authors are able not only to expose the attitudes of the missionaries and the ideology behind their actions, but also to challenge them and look at the official narrative from a different perspective. Hence, scholars in this phase (i.e., Sylvest, Martínez, Machado, and Barton) are concerned with the actions of the people and the way they structure their communities in light of their Protestant identity. From this concern, the principles of the missionary activity are confronted because the community acquires a voice and is not simply reacting to the missionaries. In these narratives the Latina/o community is the subject and protagonist of the action, as the people are in control of their own experiences. It is not a paradigm that silences the missionary activities, but that presents these activities as one aspect in the process of contact and exchange between missionaries and the Latina/o community that allows this community to generate new religious identity.

Methodologically, scholars within this phase begin to use multiple interpretative lenses beyond the simplistic descriptive analysis. Martínez uses some cultural analysis in order to identify the process of identity construction that distinguishes Mexican American Protestant culture from that of the Euro-American missionaries. On the other hand, Machado uses discourse analysis in order to deconstruct the normative discourse that has silenced and kept at the margins the voices of the Latina/o community, while also offering a different reading and interpretation of the history as it pertains the Latina/o community. Finally, Barton, while also employing cultural analysis on the construction of identity by Mexican American Protestants, goes beyond the analysis of cultural aspects. He begins looking at rituals and concrete religious experiences, like singing within worship, as the source of that development of identity outside the missionary ideology. As mentioned before, these approaches locate the Latina/o community at the center of the narratives, and the ideologies and normative discourses of those in power are challenged. It is a way of highlighting the agency of the Latina/o community.

THIRD PHASE: PARTICIPATORY ANALYSIS

As scholars leave behind the focus on missionary histories and concentrate more on the actual experiences of the people and how they allow us to reinterpret the past, the field of Latina/o Protestant history enters its third phase. In this phase, which is still in its nascent stages, scholars are interested in the construction of social and cultural histories based on sociological approaches, specifically ethnographic work. *Latino Pentecostal Identity* exemplifies this type of approach and the analysis that historians are able to do.[43]

[43] Other works that I do not examine here but that are situated within this

From interviews (oral histories) to the analysis of religious experiences (rituals and educational practices), historians are able to look at the history of these communities as a work in progress and not as an objective feature of the past. Of course traditional approaches like analysis of documents and interpretation of previous narratives are used, but the participatory analysis approach at the core of this phase provides the opportunity to look at history from a subjective perspective, that of the present protagonist of the narratives. One is able to include gender, race, and class analysis as each adds to the perspective of these protagonists who confront not only those in power within their institutions but also the oppressive systems in the society at large.

As this third phase progresses, it will be important to pay attention to the emergence of other methodological approaches that focus on participatory analysis. At the same time, it will be interesting to see if Busto's work serves as a model of connecting this field to the lager Latina/o community by using religion and religious vision as the lenses of analysis.

PARADIGMS WITHIN LATINA/O RELIGIOUS HISTORIOGRAPHY

The development of both Latina/o Catholic and Latina/o Protestant historiographies has been sustained by a constant revision of approaches. A comparison between these shows that while there are different points of development, there has been a movement in both toward the inclusion of the Latina/o community as the subject of the narratives. In this section, I compare and contrast these developments in order to provide an assessment of the state of the larger field of Latina/o religious history, specifically as it pertains to the multiplicity of methodological and theoretical approaches used.

---

phase are Daniel Ramírez' book project "Migrating Faiths: A Social and Cultural History of Pentecostalism in the United States and Mexico, 1906–1966" (unpublished manuscript); and Samuel Cruz, *Masked Africanisms: Puerto Rican Pentecostalism* (Dubuque, Iowa: Kendall Hunt, 2005). It is important to acknowledge that all of these works are on Latina/o Pentecostalism, which has not been comprehensively explored until the last decade.

DIFFERENCES

In observing the literature within both of these fields, it is obvious that the Mexican American community has been the center of most of the research, but within Latina/o Catholic historiography one finds explorations on other Latina/o groups, which it is not the case within Latina/o Protestant historiography. This can be explained by the fact that some scholars of Latina/o Catholicism have expanded their analyses beyond the Southwest region, which Latina/o Protestant historiography has not. This difference is also linked to the multiple approaches scholars within both fields have employed in their work. For example, while in the study of Latina/o Catholicism scholars have incorporated ritual or cultural analysis within a particular setting and a city, as in the case of Miami, San Antonio, and Houston, scholars of Latina/o Protestantism, with the exception of Holland's work in Los Angeles, have focused their analyses on a more regional scale. The former allows scholars also to draw on urban studies, which enhances the type of analysis done regarding the social and cultural location of the community.

Another distinction between these two fields is the fact that within Latina/o Catholic historiography we find literature that focuses on the historical religious experiences of the larger community and how they relate to the experiences within the church (i.e., Treviño and García). It is a look that provides a historical understanding of the role of religion within the larger Latina/o community and not just simply within the church, and in which religion is no longer just a system but becomes an interpretative lens. This approach locates the beginning of the analysis in the religious identities of the community in order to create the links with the activities and rituals of the church. Within Latina/o Protestant historiography, with the exception of Busto's work on Tijerina, we do not find a great deal of these cultural and social analyses that are located within the larger Latina/o community, outside the church. Here, the analysis begins in the experiences in the church and how it relates with the social agenda of that institution. The locality is the major difference between these approaches, church versus community.

SIMILARITIES

At first glance it is easy to appreciate the presence of a liberationist paradigm in both fields as the historical analyses move from the perspective of those in power to the perspective of the people, the oppressed. This paradigm followed the shifts away from the more institutional histories, in the case of Latina/o Catholic histories, and missionary histories, in the case of Latina/o Protestant histories, to focus on the religious experiences and activities of the people. In both cases, scholars began to look at religious experiences as lenses through which one should interpret the past. Hence, there is not a simple look at the events of the past in order to narrativize them, but there is interpretation of these events and the ideology behind them in light of the present experience of the people.

For example, Matovina's analysis of the Guadalupe devotion, Tweed's examination of the shrine of Our Lady of Charity and its devotion, and Sánchez Walsh's study on the development of Latina/o Pentecostal subcultures in several religious groups are works that not only focus on the experiences of the people, but that introduce the history of the community as a historical path, a journey. In this approach, the events of the past are reinterpreted through new lenses and acquire new meanings beyond the ones those in power may have imposed through normative discourses or knowledge. Part of the reason for this development of new approaches that promote the reinterpretation of the past and challenge the traditional narratives is the interest of scholars to make the case that Latina/o communities form their identities independent from those that the dominant structures try to impose.

Finally, both of these fields are connecting their discourses with other larger fields like Latina/o studies and U.S. religious studies. Scholars understand that these two fields have ignored the value of Latina/o religious histories and have not included these histories within their narratives, leaving them at the margins. Within Latina/o studies religion is not used as a interpretative tool, while within U.S. religious studies Latinas/os are not seen as actors and their voices have been silenced, turned into footnotes.

STATE OF LATINA/O RELIGIOUS HISTORIOGRAPHY

Taking into consideration the differences and similarities between the development of both Latina/o Catholic historiography and Latina/o Protestant historiography, I argue that the larger field of Latina/o religious history is going through a process of reinvention. The traditional historical approach of gathering data and organizing it as a narrative in order to merely describe an event, the act of narrativizing, is no longer the major approach within this field.

Scholars in the past decade have been engaged in participatory forms of analysis and discursive practices that provide proof of the agency of the Latina/o community and challenge the previous normative discourses. The methodologies and theories of analysis, for the most part, have come from the social sciences, like cultural studies and ethnography.

Here, I argue that what we are experiencing within Latina/o religious historiography is a sociological turn. Even when historians still depend on conventional historical tools like oral histories and archival research, the theories of analysis are coming from the social sciences. For example, approaches like lived religion, transnational and migratory analysis, and, in some cases, gender analysis are dominating the larger field of Latina/o religious studies, and their effects within historical studies are present as evidenced in many of the works I examined within these two chapters. This sociological turn, as I mentioned above, has helped open the field to new approaches, but there is always the danger that scholars may lose themselves in the history of the present, forgetting the interpretation of the past in light of the present.

In the past decade, many studies exploring Latina/o religious experiences have been done from sociological perspectives, and they have contributed to the growth of scholarship on Latina/o religions.[44] Latina/o religious historians have to be able to draw on these approaches as we explore our subjects of interest, but without falling prey to the neoliberal attitude that privileges analysis of the present over all else. In the present neoliberal condition, the system of power argues that the present supersedes the past as the essential character of history. In this sense, the present becomes history and dictates the agenda of world history, and the way people respond to this agenda.[45] In many cases in today's society, looking at the past

[44] See Alberto Pulido, *The Sacred World of the Penitentes* (Washington, D.C.: Smithsonian Institution, 2000); Luis D. León, *La Llorona's Children: Religion, Life, and Death in the U.S.-Mexican Borderlands* (Berkeley: University of California Press, 2004); and Hector Avalos, ed., *Introduction to the U.S. Latina and Latino Religious Experience* (Boston: Brill Academic, 2004).

[45] This could be exemplified through the examination of the so-called war against terrorism. The history of this "war" was written as people saw it on CNN, Fox News, MSNBC, and other networks. The present became the "history." People saw two buildings collapse. People saw revenge through the exercise of power, and that became the history. The problem is that through the glorification of the

seems like a subversive act because the structures of power are interested in the present, ignoring that the past opens a window to the understanding of that present. Because of this neoliberal approach, I fear that the field of Latina/o religious history may become obsolete as most of the interest is directed toward the religious experiences of the present. Through the use of varied methodologies and theories, we are able both to learn from the experiences of the present and to reinterpret the events of the past from multiple perspectives. Understanding these two aspects, one is able to construct historical discourses that, while incomplete, would offer a more comprehensive analysis of the past as a journey, not a finished product.

This is my task in the next section as I engage some theoretical approaches from postcolonizing perspectives offering Latina/o religious historians potential lenses of analysis and methodologies that will maintain the development of the field.

---

present, the "history" of this "war" does not take the past into consideration: the actions by the empire. People outside the centers of power have talked about that past, but since people did not see it in the "present" through the lenses of CNN or the Internet, it was silenced and ignored.

PART III

THEORIES AND METHODOLOGIES FROM A POSTCOLONIZING PERSPECTIVE

Haitian historian Michel-Rolph Trouillot asserts that "theories of history rarely examine in detail the concrete production of specific narratives."[1] Because of this lack of examination, historical narratives are usually deconstructed and reconfigured only on the basis of "facts," and not on the basis of the ideology behind their construction. In many cases the "new" versions of old historical narratives are infused with the same colonialist ideology that helped build the original versions. In order to challenge traditional historical narratives and the ideology behind them without reproducing its colonial aspect, historians need to look beyond the simple narrativizing of the story and engage theories of understanding within their work. This is why in the second part I explored the major theoretical and methodological approaches used within Latina/o religious historiography, following Trouillot's challenge of looking at narratives beyond their facts. It serves as a way of evaluating the field at its core in order to maintain its development without compromising its value as a counter-discourse.

In this third part, I examine different theoretical approaches I find to be useful in order to develop this field in two major areas: 1) Challenging and deconstructing the normative historical discourses that have dominated and/or silenced our histories; and 2) Creating subversive discourses that focus on the agency of the Latina/o community. These theoretical approaches are lived religion

[1] Michel-Rolph Trouillot, *Silencing the Past: Power and the Production of History* (Boston: Beacon, 1995), 22.

analysis, gender analysis, and migration and transnational analysis. I do not study these approaches in a vacuum, as if just their common understandings would serve perfectly the two major areas. I argue that in order for these to be useful for Latina/o religious historians, they must be seen through a postcolonizing perspective. Hence, in order to break away from the old and new hegemonies, and from the colonial perspectives embedded within the field of history, it is important to reconstruct the way we approach our task as the interpreters of the past in light of a postcolonizing project.

This postcolonizing project intends to look at history as an interpretation of the past, not as the truth about the past, in order for the subaltern to find themselves as historical subjects. In this sense, I agree with Arif Dirlik as he argues:

> For the marginalized and oppressed in particular, whose histories have been erased by power, it becomes all the more important to recapture or remake the past in their efforts to render themselves visible historically, as the very struggle to become visible presupposes a historical identity. In the face of a "historiographic colonialism" that denies them their historicity, capturing the truth of history, of oppression and the resistance to it, is a fundamental task.[2]

This is why it is important not only to dis-cover stories and memories that challenge the colonial discourse, but also to develop new ways of writing history so that voices currently in the margins may be brought to the historical process. This inclusion should not be in the form of a footnote nor should it be peripheral; instead it should be a significant part of the history and the actual process of writing that history. The approaches I explore here from a postcolonizing perspective help integrate these voices within the discourses and the writing of these discourses while at the same time challenging the colonial historical discourses.

In the first chapter of this part, I introduce and explain what I mean by a postcolonizing criticism and how this might help in the construction of subaltern histories. This chapter serves as the core of this section of the book because in it I look at the main characteristics of this theoretical approach. After this presentation, I explore

[2] Arif Dirlik, *Postmodernity's Histories: The Past as Legacy and Project* (Lanham, Md.: Rowman & Littlefield, 2000), 215–16.

two different methodological approaches that could be used in the development of subaltern histories. In chapter 6, I examine the lived religion approach and then, in chapter 7, I look at feminist criticism. While I examine each of these approaches separately, it is important to acknowledge that they are complementary to each other. In each of these chapters, I scrutinize these methodological approaches in order to provide a deeper understanding of the processes historians are able to use in their construction of historical narratives from a postcolonizing perspective. This is essential for Latina/o religious historians, as this approach would further the development of their field and continue to challenge the traditional discourse within U.S. religious history.

5 THE POSTCOLONIZING PROJECT

[T]hat effort to study the past trying to listen to those voices that have become barely audible whispers: the voices of those who were conquered and because of their defeat have in many ways been silenced and made invisible. They have been made invisible despite the historical evidence of their living and being; they have been silenced despite the historical horror of their suffering.

—Daisy Machado, "A Borderlands Perspective," 49

Historical narratives are always written from someone's or some group's perspective. That perspective usually leaves the subaltern outside the narratives.[1] Throughout time, historical narratives have been written from the perspectives of the "winners," those in power, and the subaltern has been left outside or at the margins of the narratives as addenda or footnotes. Narrating from the perspectives of the winners implies that those in power not only control the narratives but also become the subjects and actors within them. The subaltern within the narrative is an object and has no power, and thus no voice. This is the reality of the Latina/o community within the official U.S. religious discourses. It is the task of Latina/o religious history not only to give voice to those who have been silenced, but

[1] I use the term "subaltern" as it refers "to those groups in society who are subject to the hegemony of the ruling classes." Bill Ashcroft, Gareth Griffiths, and Helen Tiffin, *Post-colonial Studies: The Key Concepts* (London: Routledge, 2000), 215. In the case of my study, I argue that Latinas/os are part of the subaltern class and as such have been left out of the traditional historical narratives.

also to dismantle the narratives imposed by the "winners." Thus, it is important to see the writing of history as an inclusive and comprehensive task. As Daisy Machado argues, "In this process of looking at the past with an open and engaging mind, the historian is called upon to provide some sort of social analysis that moves beyond simply reporting past events."[2]

If there are no subversive counter-discourses, the history of those in power is then articulated as the truth and fixed as the normative knowledge. This allows history to be kidnapped by "enlightened people" and falsified appropriately so that it would be unrecognizable to *los de abajo*.[3] The falsification is done through the hiding of voices, the erasure of memory, and the isolation of any enterprises that would go beyond the "real" history to dis-cover and understand what has been concealed. Modern intellectuals determine, through obscure judgments, the fate of these enterprises and other kinds of critical thinking, by dismissing them as poetry, utopia, or fiction.[4] Counter-discourses, such as Latina/o religious histories, work to expose the falsification, to unsilence the silencing and to uncover memory. The use of different theoretical analyses helps expand the reach of this subversive agenda, and thus I argue that postcolonizing criticism is one of those theoretical approaches that would expand the methods within the field in order to challenge the normative epistemologies and generate new counter-discourses.

In this chapter, I explore postcolonizing criticism and its application within the field of history. In the first section, I engage the field of postcolonial theory in order to introduce it and contextualize its use within my project. After that, I apply postcolonizing criticism in order to challenge traditional historiography. This exercise allows us, in the next section, to look deeper into the way the subaltern is represented within traditional historiography compared to the way these representations are constructed through postcolonizing criticism. In the last section, I move to analyze the way subaltern

[2] Daisy Machado, "A Borderlands Perspective," in *Hidden Stories: Unveiling the History of the Latino Church*, ed. Daniel R. Rodríguez-Díaz and David Cortés-Fuentes (Decatur, Ga.: Asociación para la Educación Teológica Hispana, 1994), 49–50.

[3] Subcomandante Marcos, *Los del Color de la Tierra: Textos Insurgentes* (Nafarroa, Spain: Txalaparta, 2001), 18.

[4] Marcos, *Los del Color*, 18.

histories are constructed as subversive discourses using a postcolonizing approach. It is important to establish that I do not discuss every debate within the field of postcolonial studies, as my interest is to introduce it as a theoretical approach within our historical task.[5]

WHY POSTCOLONIZING CRITICISM?

Many scholars agree that the "field" of postcolonial studies traces its origins to the publication of the book *Orientalism* by Edward W. Said in 1978, without disregarding its connections to earlier works by Frantz Fanon and Albert Memmi.[6] In the present, no one can claim that postcolonial studies are contained within a single discipline or program.[7] While most of the work has been done in English departments and within literary criticism, postcolonial studies have

[5] One of these debates has to do with the discussion on the term postcolonialism and its linguistic reference to the end of postcolonialism. See Anne McClintock, "The Angel of Progress: Pitfalls of the Term 'Postcolonialism,'" in *Colonial Discourse/Postcolonial Theory*, ed. Francis Barker, Peter Hulme, and Margaret Iversen (Manchester, UK: Manchester University Press, 1994); Ella Shohat, "Notes on the 'Post-colonial,'" in *Contemporary Postcolonial Theory: A Reader*, ed. Padmini Mongia (London: Arnold, 1996); Arif Dirlik, *The Postcolonial Aura: Third World Criticism in the Age of Global Capitalism* (Boulder, Colo.: Westview, 1997); and Ruth Frankenberg and Lata Mani, "Crosscurrents, Crosstalk: Race, 'Postcoloniality' and the Politics of Location," in Mongia, *Contemporary Postcolonial Theory*. While the totality of this discussion lies beyond the scope of my project, it is important to acknowledge that I do take a stand within it by constantly using the term postcolonizing, instead of postcolonial or postcolonialism. The term postcolonizing, as I use it, implies a temporal movement, a process, beyond the condition of colonialism. Here, I agree with Ato Quayson, who talks about postcolonizing instead of postcolonialism (*Postcolonialism: Theory, Practice or Process?* [Cambridge, UK: Polity, 2000]). This change in terminology is essential because through the use of postcolonizing I am arguing that people who are no longer politically colonized but have adopted or internalized the imperial discourses need also to immerse in the process of postcolonization. Postcolonizing implies a movement toward a goal, which entails the reinterpretation of one's past and the reconstruction of an identity. I use the term postcolonial only as I refer to the name of the field, postcolonial theory.

[6] Edward W. Said, *Orientalism* (New York: Vintage, 1978); Frantz Fanon, *The Wretched of the Earth* (New York: Grover, 1963); and Albert Memmi, *The Colonizer and the Colonized* (Boston: Beacon, 1965).

[7] Jenny Sharpe, "Postcolonial Studies in the House of US Multiculturalism," in *A Companion to Postcolonial Studies*, ed. Henry Schwarz and Sangeeta Ray (Malden, Mass.: Blackwell, 2000), 112.

challenged disciplines such as political science, law, sociology, and history, just to mention a few. Of course, every discipline has used postcolonizing criticism for its own benefit and agenda. In this sense the effort of explaining and defining the status of these theories of analysis turns out to be an unfeasible task. And as Sara Castro-Klaren argues, "Postcolonial theory is by no means a set of coherent and integrated approaches, assumptions, or methods in cultural analysis, but it has been an exceptionally important institutional development in the English-speaking world."[8] Thus, for this project, I examine postcolonizing criticism as it deals with the reconstruction of historical discourses, although I recognize its diversity of uses in various disciplines.

Postcolonizing criticism has allowed scholars to examine and critique colonial discourses and to reconstruct the history of the subaltern. Colonial discourse analysis and postmodern theory are at the center of the development of postcolonizing criticism. Through discourse analysis we are able to explore the ways in which subaltern histories are kept hidden by the modes of representation, like narritivizing. The dismantling of colonial discourses breaks the representations of the subaltern supported by those in power. Thus, not only does this type of analysis examine the way these discourses are produced and the ideologies behind them, but it also challenges the knowledge that comes out of them, which is presented as truth. Again, Castro-Klaren's argument proves essential in explaining my use of postcolonizing criticism:

> Postcolonial theory, in all its heterogeneity and ambition, redeploys key aspects in postmodern theory—opacity of language, decentering of the subject, suspicion of authority, demolition of epistemological and cultural universal claims, relocation of subjects—in order to show the complicity of "knowledge" and systems of imperial domination.[9]

[8] Sara Castro-Klaren, "Posting Letters: Writing in the Andes and the Paradoxes of the Postcolonial Debate," in *Coloniality at Large: Latin America and the Postcolonial Debate,* ed. Mabel Moraña, Enrique Dussel, and Carlos A. Jáuregui (Durham, N.C.: Duke University Press, 2008), 135.

[9] Castro-Klaren, "Posting Letters," 135–36.

It is in this sense that I believe postcolonial theory works together with Foucault's own discourse theory and on the basis of this understanding, I use postcolonizing criticism to explore historiography.

POSTCOLONIZING TRADITIONAL HISTORY

Traditional historiography represents a colonial enterprise. It develops historical narratives that marginalize the subaltern class by silencing their voices and erasing their memory. These historical narratives become colonial discourses while at the same time becoming universal and normative. These histories are written based on power, and one of their purposes is to establish control over the subaltern. By controlling their history, which tends to be seen as the actual past, those in power control the present and the future of the subaltern. Hence, as Frantz Fanon tells us, "Colonialism is not satisfied merely with holding people in its grip and emptying the native's brain of all form and content. By a kind of perverted logic, it turns to the past of the oppressed people, and distorts, disfigures, and destroys it."[10] Colonial discourses work on two levels: 1) They promote a universal history and knowledge in which the subaltern is silenced and oppressed; and 2) They maintain the representations that support the idea of the subaltern without a history outside the one imposed by the normative history.[11] This normative history becomes a grand history, a metanarrative through which everything else should be understood, and as such it should deconstructed.

BREAKING THE GRAND NARRATIVES

Michel Foucault contributes to the critique of these grand narratives with an opposition to the premise that *total* history can be achieved. He argues that this kind of history has been based on continuity and linear successions, but that it is time to turn attention to the discontinuities and disruptions. Historians have to look at the past to find *monuments* (his term) and tie them together into totalities. In this process, other *monuments* are left behind because they break

[10] Frantz Fanon, *The Wretched of the Earth* (New York: Grover, 1963), 210.

[11] The dominant religious history of the U.S. Southwest fits this colonialist approach, as it has been written on the basis of the "frontier thesis" and its myth of the empty land. These colonial discourses distort the past, erasing the racist attitudes, the violence, and the domination of the missionary activities. Thus, Latinas/os—specifically in this case, the Mexican and Mexican American—are left out of the discourse and their past is hidden.

the unity of the narrative, and it is in these monuments that we find subaltern histories, which represent discontinuities. In this regard, Foucault differentiates between *total* history and *general* history, the second project being the task for new historians. "The project of a *total* history is one that seeks to reconstitute the overall form of a civilization, the principle—material or spiritual—of a society, the significance common to all the phenomena of a period, the law that accounts for their cohesion—what is called metaphorically the 'face' of a period."[12] *General* history, on the other hand, focuses on the correlation between the phenomena, not to draw them together as *total* history does but to "deploy the space of a dispersion."[13] This is closely related to Walter Benjamin's argument of looking at moments in history for what they are, and not only for their connections to other moments. Even further, Benjamin argues that it is essential to look for the disconnections between these moments. It is a method of looking at the discontinuities in history.[14]

Traditional history, following a modernist impulse, pursued the project of *total* history, which led to universal history, in order to organize events together into one narrative, as if the past itself was reproduced. Foucault rejected this idea because history was a continuous work of interpretation by the historian, and her/his own presuppositions and imagination became part of history in the process. This argument of historical interpretation became a direct rejection of the possibility of objectivity; for Foucault this also meant questioning the relationship between power and knowledge: Significantly, he saw knowledge and power as inextricably connected. In particular, there are no 'truths' but only official or dominant knowledges which impart power to those who know and speak

[12] Michel Foucault, *The Archaeology of Knowledge & the Discourse on Language,* trans. A. M. Sheridan Smith (New York: Pantheon, 1972), 9 (emphasis in original).

[13] Foucault, *Archaeology of Knowledge,* 10.

[14] Walter Benjamin, "Theses on the Philosophy of History," in *Illuminations,* ed. Hannah Arendt, trans. Harry Zohn (New York: Schocken, 1985), 253–64. For some analysis on Benjamin's argument, see Hjamil A. Martínez-Vázquez, "Breaking the Established Scaffold: Imagination as a Resource in the Development of Biblical Interpretation," in *Her Master's Tools? Feminist and Post-colonial Engagements of Historical-Critical Discourse,* SBL Global Perspectives on the Bible 9, ed. Todd Penner and Caroline Vander Stichele (Atlanta: Society of Biblical Literature, 2005), 71–91.

them."[15] In traditional history, power is exercised when voices and stories (*monuments*) are left hidden in the grand narratives that assume a universal knowledge. Michel-Rolph Trouillot goes further to argue that, within the public's sense of history,

> The role of the historian is to reveal the past, to discover or, at least, approximate the truth. Within that viewpoint, power is unproblematic, irrelevant to the construction of the narrative as such. At best, history is a story about power, a story about those who won.[16]

To uncover the power/knowledge paradigm, Foucault proposed archaeology and genealogy as the methods to reveal the constructions of discourses in relation to the present experience. Following Foucault's method, historians are challenged to confront traditional historiography and to focus their work on the marginal, which is peripheral to the centers of power, by understanding the grand narratives and uncovering the power embedded in them.

Jacques Derrida, like Foucault, articulates a critique to the modernist project. Derrida is usually associated with deconstruction and poststructuralism, and both of these concepts/movements are connected to the linguistic turn in history. Derrida argues that, through the process of deconstruction of texts, established meanings and organizing truths are challenged. This process exposes the modernist project. Deconstruction asserts that there is no fixed or universal meaning or truth, since the author or speaker does not provide "privileged or fixed origin for meaning."[17] For history, this means that there is no direct contact with the past; the past is a text in itself that needs interpretation. Texts are full of different meanings, and every interpretation is already "conditioned by past interpretations as well as our present conditions."[18] Thus, history cannot claim any

[15] See Michel Foucault, *Power/Knowledge: Selected Interviews and Other Writings, 1972–1977*, ed. Colin Gordon, trans. Colin Gordon, Leo Marshall, John Mepham, and Kate Soper (New York: Pantheon, 1980).

[16] Michel-Rolph Trouillot, *Silencing the Past: Power and the Production of History* (Boston: Beacon, 1995), 5.

[17] Alan Munslow, *The Routledge Companion to Historical Studies* (London: Routledge, 2000), 74.

[18] Anna Green and Kathleen Troup, *The Houses of History: A Critical Reader in Twentieth-Century History and Theory* (New York: New York University Press, 1999), 299.

fixed meaning or truth about the past because the author plays an important role and she/he cannot claim objectivity. Anna Green and Kathleen Troup summarize this challenge to traditional history as follows:

> If the meaning of a text is necessarily uncertain, how much more problematic are the historical facts constructed from that text. Facts cannot be independent, and representative of an external reality: they are already historicized, their "truth" indeterminable. Thus it is not possible to verify another historian's interpretation by reference to the facts; all we can do is re-read an (open) text.[19]

Derrida focuses his work on the analysis of language. Here, he connects to poststructuralism, which reacts against structuralism and proposes that it is through language that power is exercised. This movement calls for the erasure of binary opposition, which is part of Western logic, since the one who creates these oppositions is the one with the power. For example, in the creation of the opposition man/woman, it is the man who has exercised power in order to produce a representation of what a woman should be for his own benefit of maintaining control over her. Categories like man and woman are not as transparent as their construction through binary opposition might argue. Breaking these oppositions opens the door for redefinitions of cultural concepts without insisting on any fixed meaning. "Contests about meaning involve the introduction of new oppositions, the reversal of hierarchies, the attempt to expose repressed terms, to challenge the natural status of seemingly dichotomous pairs, and to expose their interdependence and their internal instability."[20] Since traditional academic institutionalized history has participated in the perpetuation of fixed meanings, it is important to confront and reject these in order to open up the path for new interpretations without any trace or desire for universal recognition. Thus, historians become aware of the limits of their historical discourses and recognize the presence of a multiplicity of voices and histories.

[19] Green and Troup, *Houses of History,* 299.

[20] Joan Wallach Scott, *Gender and the Politics of History* (New York: Columbia University Press, 1999), 7.

BRINGING THEORY BACK: HISTORY AS REPRESENTATION

Both theoretical projects, Foucault's and Derrida's, open the field of history to the discussion of theory within it. I understand theory, in this case, as a paradigm of knowledge, a model, and not as a hypothesis. Theory allows the questioning of the rules and practices being used in academic institutionalized history and its exclusive character in the representation of knowledge about the past. These questionings engage history in its content and form, exposing historical discourses as representations of the past, not the ultimate truth. Now, these theoretical approaches need to confront the dominant scaffold, not support it. These theoretical tools bring oppositional ideology to the writing of history and open the space for difference.

Postcolonizing theory emerges from the perspective of the subaltern, a theory based on the experiences of struggle and resistance of those living in the margins. It thus lies outside the scope of the discourses taking place in dominant academic circles. It talks back to these circles, confronting them with new meanings, new stories, and new voices. Sonia Saldívar-Hull points out this argument as she states:

> Hegemony has so constructed the ideas of method and theory that often we cannot recognize anything that is different from what the dominant discourse constructs. As a consequence, we have to look in nontraditional places for our theories: in the prefaces to anthologies, in the interstices of autobiographies, in our cultural artifacts (the cuentos), and, if we are fortunate enough to have access to a good library, in the essays published in marginalized journals not widely distributed by the dominant institutions.[21]

From the perspective of the subaltern, the use of theories provides us with new categories and definitions that help in the task of confronting the normative discourse and constructing new counter-discourses. These theories have to guide the writing of the narratives. In order to be a genuine counter-discourse, this writing has to be "as *self*-critical as it is critical of others."[22] By self-critical, I am arguing

[21] See Sonia Saldívar-Hull, *Feminism on the Border: Chicana Gender Politics and Literature* (Berkeley: University of California Press, 2000), 46.

[22] Hayden White, *Tropics of Discourse: Essays in Cultural Criticism* (Baltimore: Johns Hopkins University Press, 1978), 4 (emphasis in original).

that the discourse understands itself as a discourse and not as the ultimate truth.

Until the postmodern turn to theory, the majority of historians looked at the past by means of archives and other documents in order to ascertain particular facts and build a coherent narrative, which served in the understanding of that past. Theory had not become an integral part of the discipline of history.[23] After Leopold von Ranke's propositions for the shaping of the discipline, with a theory and a method that endorsed the centrality of Europe and promoted the project of universal history, many historians have not felt it necessary to talk about their particular approach and the scaffold to their work, their theory.[24] Without this aspect, historians are not able to look beyond the narratives (stories) into the scaffolds of the narratives. Openness to theory would allow a deconstruction and reconstruction of these scaffolds, and such openness "changes the archive, alters the record, and reconfigures the facts."[25] In this regard, Keith Jenkins argues that "history is theoretical 'all the way down,' and that all history students should not only consider the question of the nature of history/historiography in its various ontological, epistemological, methodological and ideological/discursive manifestations, but that they should be especially aware of that theorizing which currently lives under the rubric of postmodernism."[26] Theory plays a definitive function in the interpretation of the facts, so including it as part of history would expose the presuppositions and biases of the

[23] Theory, ultimately, determines which authors are considered and what counts as an established fact. I am proposing a theory that steps away from the modern/colonial perspective of the centrality of Europe. This theory will question every account and "fact" to uncover its roots, the ideology behind its creation, and its purpose. In other words, through the use of theory silences can be exposed, even if they are still missing from the historical account.

[24] For a better understanding of Ranke's vision, see Leopold von Ranke, *The Theory and the Practice of History*, ed. Georg G. Iggers and Konrad von Moltke, trans. Wilma A. Iggers and Konrad von Moltke (Indianapolis: Bobbs-Merrill, 1973); and Georg G. Iggers and James M. Powell, eds., *Leopold von Ranke and the Shaping of the Historical Discipline* (Syracuse, N.Y.: Syracuse University Press, 1990).

[25] Mark Poster, *Cultural History and Postmodernity: Disciplinary Readings and Challenges* (New York: Columbia University Press, 1997), 157.

[26] Keith Jenkins, "Introduction: On Being Open about Our Closures," in *The Postmodern History Reader*, ed. Keith Jenkins (London: Routledge, 1997), 1–2.

historian. Thus, the historical account would be more coherent and the ideological aspects would be revealed up front. It would confront traditional historiography, and it would help us to *think* about the past, rather than to continue *investigating* it.[27]

Feminist history offers a great example of this openness to theory. This field has accepted its own political and ideological stance by critiquing modern historiography and its characterizations of gender. Feminist historians have continued the work of recovering voices but have included a look at the theory and methodology behind their task. Postmodern historians have done the same thing by using Foucault and Derrida in order to restructure the discipline of history and have seen in feminist history a big step forward. However, the reality is that these kinds of approaches are not present in the majority of historical work, especially within U.S. religious historical studies. Religious historians do not constantly evaluate their task and the condition of their discipline. This has led to a critical separation of historians from the present situation. Many have critiqued postmodernism and poststructuralism by arguing that its attention to texts as well as theory disregards the importance of experiences and agency in historical writing. But again, feminist history proves this wrong with its approach to theory and agency at the same time.

Ignoring theory has led to the continuation and perpetuation of the status quo in the discipline of religious history. Historians, following the project of traditional historiography, are not auto-referential of their own theoretical presuppositions and scaffolds, leaving the discussion of theory outside their own discourse and perpetuating the same agenda of Western modern historical discourse. As mentioned above, the idea of achieving truth, which becomes universal, is still the main force behind religious historical writing, which proves that the modernist agenda is still present in the discipline today. Truth about the past cannot be attained in the writing of history since, as Walter Benjamin acknowledges, "the true picture of the past flits by."[28] History is the representation (*mimēsis*) or construction of the past through narrative. In talking about the knowledge that comes out of these discourses, Kelvin A. Santiago-Valles

[27] F. R. Ankersmit, "History and Postmodernism," in Jenkins, *Postmodern History Reader*, 283–84, reprinted from *History and Theory* 28 (1989): 294.

[28] Benjamin, "Theses," 255.

finds that "knowledge of the past, then, is doubly representational: the past appears again (re-presents itself) in the present, and this re-apparition can only materialize in the shape of an approximation-in-thought that substitutes the original past (re-presents it)."[29] These representations and constructions are embedded within the ideological and political agendas of the authors. One needs to argue that historical discourses as representational knowledge do not provide an absolute truth, but an interpretation. Thus, objectivity cannot be achieved in historical writing since it is superseded by subjectivity.

Historians look at the evidence about the past in the form of documents, artifacts, and other sources, which are already filtered through the interpretation of someone in the past. Then, they interpret this evidence with their own glasses and imagine a story that links all the evidence together through a process of emplotment. The final product of this process is not "what actually happened" in the past, nor is it the past itself, but a representation of the past, a construction or reconstruction of the past, through the eyes of an individual.[30] Most historians have been conscious of this process of interpretation and representation, but have still maintained a search for truth with a sense of objectivity. The absence of theory in their work prevents them from acknowledging their own participation in the modernist project of universalizing knowledge and history, and takes away the particularity of a moment in time, which can serve as "a revolutionary chance in the fight for the oppressed past."[31] In other words, this approach erases the possibility of alternative knowledge and the opportunity for the non-European alterity to tell their side of the story by dis-covering their evidence and *monuments* of the past and locating them outside the confines of that which is called *truth*.

[29] Kelvin A. Santiago-Valles, *"Subject People" and Colonial Discourses: Economic Transformation and Social Disorder in Puerto Rico, 1898–1947* (Albany: State University of New York Press, 1994), 9.

[30] For an in-depth discussion on the nature of historical narratives, see Hayden White, *Metahistory: The Historical Imagination in Nineteenth-Century Europe* (Baltimore: Johns Hopkins University Press, 1973); and Hayden White, *The Content of the Form: Narrative Discourse and Historical Representation* (Baltimore: Johns Hopkins University Press, 1987).

[31] Benjamin, "Theses," 263.

Postcolonizing criticism, through the openness to theory, breaks down these understandings of historical narratives as the actual past and conveyers of truth. It exposes these discourses as representations of the past and thus allows for the interest in looking at what is left out, at the "discontinuities" of the discourse. Within these discontinuities one finds the subaltern, who is left out, silenced within colonial discourses such as the ones traditional historiography has produced. The inclusion of theory (discourse analysis and feminist analysis) provides the foundation for the deconstruction of these colonial discourses, and thus the silences are "unsilenced" and recognized, providing the location of the gaps (discontinuities) in the narrative. As Emma Pérez argues, "These interstitial gaps interrupt the linear model of time, and it is in such locations that oppositional, subaltern histories can be found," and "these silences, when heard, become the negotiating spaces for the decolonizing subject."[32] Subaltern voices, memories, and stories are found in these spaces. Once dis-covered, the subaltern acquires agency within the construction of counter-narratives that traditional historiography has failed to acknowledge.[33]

FINDING THE SUBALTERN

Historical narratives, as explained above, are constructed based on representations of the events of the past and the actors of these events. But not all actors are represented as subjects of their own actions, as many groups outside the centers of power are represented as objects (recipients). Postcolonizing criticism facilitates

[32] Emma Pérez, *The Decolonial Imaginary: Writing Chicanas into History* (Bloomington: Indiana University Press, 1999), 5.

[33] Here, it is important to acknowledge the critical contribution the work of the Subaltern Studies group has provided in the development of postcolonizing criticism and the shift in the revision and reconstruction of historical narratives. In her "Subaltern Studies: Deconstructing Historiography," Gayatri Chakravorty Spivak explains the multiple ways the work of this group has contributed to the deconstruction of traditional historiography. She focuses on the revision to the perspective of looking at history using what she refers to as a theory of change. Spivak states that, "The most significant outcome of this revision or shift in perspective is that the agency of change is located in the insurgent or the 'subaltern.'" Spivak, "Subaltern Studies: Deconstructing Historiography," in *Selected Subaltern Studies*, ed. Ranajit Guha and Gayatri Chakravorty Spivak (New York: Oxford University Press, 1988), 3.

the deconstruction of these narratives, which then allows for the representation of the subaltern as an agent of her/his own history. The reconstruction of the representation of the subaltern entails the recreation of the subaltern's past and the reconstruction of their identities. The subaltern's identities, which in many cases have been fixed and essentialized by the colonial discourses, are deconstructed and reimagined, but not in a fixed way since through postcolonizing criticism they are conceived as a process. I agree with Stuart Hall as he argues:

> It is not something which already exists, transcending place, time, history and culture. Cultural identities come from somewhere, have histories. But, like everything which is historical, they undergo constant transformation. Far from being eternally fixed in some essentialized past, they are subject to the continuous "play" of history, culture and power. Far from being grounded in a "mere" recovery of the past, which is waiting to be found, and which, when found, will secure our sense of ourselves into eternity, identities are the names we give to the different ways we are positioned by, and position ourselves within, the narratives of the past.[34]

Reconstructing these identities is essential because through this process one can distinguish the subaltern as a subject through time, not as an object stuck in a particular time in the past.

SUBALTERN AS HYBRID

Because these identities are not fixed or pure, it is important to understand them in light of their multiple historical representations. Through postcolonizing criticism, the subaltern's identities are revealed as hybrid, which "refers to the creation of new transcultural forms within the contact zone produced by colonization."[35] Hybridity does not take place only in one way or in one place in particular since the contact and exchange between the subaltern and those in power occurs in different settings and many forms. The contact and exchange between the Latina/o community and Euro-American missionaries serves as one of those contact zones. Of

[34] Stuart Hall, "Cultural Identity and Diaspora," in Mongia, *Contemporary Postcolonial Theory*, 112.

[35] Ashcroft, Griffiths, and Tiffin, *Post-colonial Studies*, 118.

course, the existing Latina/o cultural identities at the time of contact were already hybrid as the result of the conquest of the Americas. Reconstructing the historical representations that explain these subaltern hybrid identities help us break away from the traditional understandings of identities as pure. Let me speak a little bit about this concept of hybridity and my own understanding of its importance within postcolonizing criticism.

Terms such as syncretism, *mestizaje, mulatez,* and creole have been associated with hybridity since they refer to contact and exchange, but within the field of postcolonial studies, hybridity has been the term that has caught scholars' imagination. Many postcolonial scholars use the term to reject the idea of the possibility of essential pre-colonial culture. Hybridity, because of this transformation in cultural identity, locates the subaltern in a different place, an "in-between" space. The "in-between" means not being in either the pre-contact cultural space (e.g., Latin American culture) or the culture of those in power (e.g., Euro-American culture); it is the formation of what Homi Bhabha has called the Third Space of enunciation. In this space, culture and meanings are not seen as pure and fixed since it is exactly the condition of "in-betweenness" that produces the realization that there can be no pure culture. Bhabha argues, "It is that Third Space, though unrepresentable in itself, which constitutes the discursive conditions of enunciation that ensure that the meaning and symbols of culture have no primordial unity or fixity; that even the same signs can be appropriated, translated, rehistoricized and read anew."[36] The subaltern finds ways to reinterpret the past from this Third Space.

I understand that some within postcolonial studies have spoken about hybridity as an all-encompassing concept to which every subaltern subscribes. The problem here resides in the lack of understanding of locality and particularity that "fails to discriminate between the diverse modalities of hybridity, for example, forced assimilation, internalized self-rejection, political cooptation, social conformism, cultural mimicry, and creative transcendence."[37] So hybridity as proposed by Bhabha and others is important in the sense that it assists the whole process of resistance of the dispossessed against the center of power, but at the same time it is dangerous because in it

[36] Homi Bhabha, *The Location of Culture* (London: Routledge, 1994), 37.
[37] Shohat, "Notes," 331.

differences are diluted and locations are not necessarily established. In other words, the danger is that the use of hybridity may homogenize the subaltern if it does not take into consideration the connections between the new identities and old national identities. The risk of universalizing the subaltern is what a concept like hybridity wants to avoid, namely, essentializing culture. By talking about hybridity without paying attention to the sources of that condition and making it a catch-all term, hybridity is equally essentialized and fixed since it gives little emphasis to the spatial and temporal. This is problematic in the sense that it leaves without any critical engagement the particular condition of hybridity, especially those instances where people through assimilation or integration do not see this condition as a significant circumstance in the process of postcolonizing. In these cases the construction of identity becomes a nonintegrated process that seems to be unchallenged by those involved in the process. As shown in the next chapter, religious experiences allow for these connections, so the hybridity I am referring to here is based on the process of cultural identities being in constant development.

Hybridity takes into consideration the location of the subaltern as a subject whose identities are always in transition, not static within a particular essential identity and fixed in the past.[38] At the same time, it is important to call attention to the danger in the use of this concept since it tends to dismiss the richness of the past prior to conquest and often does not consider that past as a source of survival for some communities as "part of the fight against continuing forms of annihilation."[39] Again, this is not to say that there is a fixed identity in the past, but rather that the past should not be dismissed from the consideration of the construction of hybrid identities. For example, as we will see in the next chapter, the construction of Latina/o identities through religious experiences cannot be comprehended without an understanding of the colonial past in Latin America and the most recent past of totalitarian governments, even though it may seem traumatic and fragmented. The collective (and individual) memory does not erase the events of the past, even if they are "covered" by new memories. Thus, as Ella Shohat proposes, "For communities which have undergone brutal ruptures, now in the process of forging a collective identity, no matter how hybrid

[38] Shohat, "Notes," 329.

[39] Shohat, "Notes," 331.

that identity has been before, during, and after colonialism, the retrieval and reinscription of a fragmented past becomes a crucial contemporary site for forging a resistant collective identity."[40]

REPRESENTATIONS OF THE SUBALTERN

This past is not understood as the clean and organized narrative that traditional historiography presents, but it is interpreted in new ways and offers the possibility of researching the past in an effort to construct more localized collective identities in order to provide resistance to specific forms of oppression. This dis-covery of the past allows the initiation of a process of self-identification disassociated from the fixed labels embedded within the traditional colonial discourses. History, thus, becomes an intrinsic aspect of the process of identity construction and of the understanding of hybrid identities in a nonessentialized way, within an "in-between" nonfixed state. Through postcolonizing criticism this "in-betweenness" is exposed, which in itself breaks the official narratives by revealing their discontinuities. As mentioned before, it is in these gaps that the subaltern is found. But it is also in the dis-covery of these discontinuities that the subaltern's consciousness is revealed so that the past can be remembered. As I have mentioned in a previous work, the importance of the act of remembering is not a matter of simply adding new data to particular normative narratives, but a matter of "dis-covering new meanings and memories that transpire by exposing the discontinuities of the normative narratives."[41] The new meanings are constructed from the perspective of the subaltern.

For the historian, the task is clear: to deconstruct the traditional narratives and recreate historical narratives that open the subaltern's consciousness to remember in order to construct their identities. This subaltern consciousness, as Spivak argues, "is not consciousness-in-general, but a historicized political species."[42] It is hard to reach it within traditional historiography because of the fragmentation of the past, but through non-modern approaches like religious experiences, the subaltern is able to make connections

[40] Shohat, "Notes," 330.

[41] Hjamil A. Martínez-Vázquez, *Latina/o y Musulmán: The Construction of Latina/o Identity among Latina/o Muslims in the United States* (Eugene, Ore.: Pickwick, 2010), 85.

[42] Spivak, "Subaltern Studies," 11.

to the past. Postcolonizing criticism is an instrument to reconstruct the representations of the past within the discursive field. These new representations offer historicity to the subaltern consciousness, and thus the subaltern acquires subjectivity within these counter-narratives. But in doing so, historians run the risk of reconstructing these representations as fixed, which would "inevitably objectify the subaltern."[43] To break away from this danger, historians need to put the subaltern at the center of the narratives in which they are actors.

This focus does not mean that the representations of the subaltern are the ultimate truth, but rather that these representations are multiple and diverse. The subaltern is represented as a subject who has defined his/her own identity recognizing the sociopolitical location. But, even then, it is important to acknowledge that there is a difference between the actual subaltern and the one represented in historical narratives. Postcolonizing criticism does not contend that the representations *are* the subaltern, which distinguishes this theory from the positivist modern approach that traditional historiography follows. Here, I am arguing that even from a postcolonizing perspective, history is still an interpretation. The difference is that within this approach the subaltern is not silent, as even a representation offers subjectivity.

Of course, if history is still done from a positivist perspective, "this subject can only be spoken for and spoken of by the transition narrative, which will ultimately privilege the modern (that is, 'Europe')."[44] This is why it is important that these new historical discourses, from the perspective of the subaltern, are constructed outside the traditional centers of power, because if they are not, they will be just reproducing the same ideology behind traditional historiography without actually challenging it. Dipesh Chakrabarty's warning on this issue is essential:

> So long as one operates within the discourse of "history" produced at the institutional site of the university, it is not possible simply to walk out of the deep collusion between "history" and the modernizing narrative(s) of citizenship, bourgeois public and private,

[43] Spivak, "Subaltern Studies," 16.

[44] Dipesh Chakrabarty, *Provincializing Europe: Postcolonial Thought and Historical Difference* (Princeton, N.J.: Princeton University Press, 2000), 41.

> and the nation state. "History" as a knowledge system is firmly embedded in institutional practices that invoke the nation-state at every step—witness the organization and politics of teaching, recruitment, promotions, and publication in history departments, politics that survive the occasional brave and heroic attempts by individual historians to liberate "history" from the metanarrative of the nation state.[45]

Thus, subaltern histories have to "liberate" the subaltern from the representations of the colonial discourses by breaking away from the positivist modern approaches traditional historiography follows. This is especially relevant as a look to the past shows that the subaltern's activities, such as their religious experiences, challenge the traditional ways of narrativizing because they cannot always be put together as one clean narrative.

SUBALTERN HISTORIES

The construction of subaltern histories depends on the ability of the historian actually to explore these activities of the subaltern, because in most cases these records cannot be found in the archives or historical texts. As Chakrabarty states, "Historians of peasants and other subaltern social groups have long emphasized the fact that peasants do not leave their own documents."[46] Historians following postcolonizing criticism are then compelled not only to look at the discontinuities and silences within the traditional narratives, but also to explore these in order to find the experiences of the subaltern, which offer some perspective of the subaltern's past.[47] These experiences, as mentioned above, cannot always be understood within a positivist modern approach, and it is because of this that subaltern histories are constructed outside the modern. The methods and theories of traditional historiography cannot grasp the subaltern's consciousness.

[45] Chakrabarty, *Provincializing Europe*, 41.

[46] Dipesh Chakrabarty, "A Small History of Subaltern Studies," in Schwarz and Ray, *Companion to Postcolonial Studies*, 47.

[47] This two-step process is what I have referred to in the past as the postcolonizing project, which consists of confrontation and dis-covery. For a comprehensive description of this project, see Hjamil A. Martínez-Vázquez, "The Postcolonizing Project: Constructing a Decolonial Imaginary from the Borderlands," *Journal of World Christianity* 1, no. 2 (2009): 1–28.

This shortcoming is especially present as one focuses on the religious experiences of the subaltern as the space of agency. The scientific and purist aspect of traditional historiography cannot grasp the multiplicity and heterogeneity of this subaltern space. What I am arguing is that the subaltern's consciousness embedded within religious practices cannot be explained through the traditional forms of representations since this consciousness is not fixed in one way or another but is always being constructed. Religious experiences allow the subaltern to remember and reconstruct the past based on the discontinuities of the silences that are now exposed. Traditional historical approaches are not concerned with multiple histories but with the construction and support of one metanarrative. Hence, a historian is not able to reach these subaltern consciousnesses with the use of the same official historical tools. Even further, as Chakrabarty states, "The practice of subaltern history would aim to take history, the code, to its limits in order to make its unworking visible."[48]

By making the subaltern the agent of the discourses, subaltern histories look into places and events that traditional historical discourses have designated as unimportant and which, in many cases, have been forgotten. It is a way of examining the past beyond what has been essentialized and fixed, and thus the exercise of writing subaltern histories becomes a subversive practice. Of course, as mentioned earlier in this chapter, these examinations of the past are translated into representations, but in subaltern histories the past is understood differently, not as something that can be objectified but lived.

> Pasts are there in taste, in practices of embodiment, in the cultural training the senses have received over generations. They are there in practices I sometimes do not even know I engage in. This is how the archaic comes into the modern, not as a remnant of another time but as something constitutive of the present.[49]

Thus, to write subaltern history is to explore the experiences and actions of the subaltern, as it is within these that we can identify the historical consciousness that opens a window to the interpretation of the subaltern's past. It is a matter of looking beyond the documents and texts that in many cases have been formed and kept by those in power.

[48] Chakrabarty, *Provincializing Europe*, 96.
[49] Chakrabarty, *Provincializing Europe*, 251.

Furthermore, most of the subaltern's actions represent concrete subversive activities against the system that marginalize their voices. Through postcolonizing criticism, subaltern histories expose these activities as counter-discourses and the subaltern "as historical subject and agent of an oppositional discourse."[50] This is another signal that not only is the knowledge produced by subaltern histories different from the one generated by traditional historical discourses, it is also confrontational to the latter one. By focusing on the subaltern, these counter-discourses do not follow the positivist modernist approach of arguing for an ultimate truth. Subaltern histories reposition the representations of the subject within historical narratives (e.g., the subaltern as agent), and provide a new understanding of the historical field.

To actually produce change, we need new discourses that discover new perspectives and voices. But, even further, we need discourses that confront traditional colonial discourses in order to dismantle them and construct new theories from a postcolonizing perspective, which can open the interpretation to all groups of society. Thinking from the subaltern's and not from the modernist perspective serves historians in both of these tasks of confronting and dis-covery. This is what Walter D. Mignolo refers to as border epistemology or subaltern knowledge.[51] Subaltern knowledges are the responses to the propositions of a universal value supported by modernity. Mignolo suggests "that subaltern reason be understood as a diverse set of theoretical practices emerging *from* and responding *to* colonial legacies at the intersection of Euro/American modern history."[52]

The subaltern constructs these theoretical practices as part of the daily struggle against coloniality, and postcolonizing criticism, with its openness to theory, is developed through the use of these theories. Now, as Mignolo acknowledges, "we should be able to distinguish *postcolonial theories* as an academic commodity (in the same way that postmodern theories were and are commodified), from

[50] Benita Parry, "Problems in Current Theories of Colonial Discourse," in *The Post-colonial Studies Reader*, ed. Bill Ashcroft, Gareth Griffiths, and Helen Tiffin (London: Routledge, 1995), 44.

[51] See Walter D. Mignolo, *Local Histories/Global Designs: Coloniality, Subaltern Knowledges, and Border Thinking* (Princeton, N.J.: Princeton University Press, 2000).

[52] Mignolo, *Local Histories*, 95 (emphasis in original).

postcolonial theorizing, as critiques subsumed under subaltern reason and border gnosis: a thinking process in which people living under colonial domination had to enact in order to negotiate their life and subaltern condition."[53] Subaltern histories, in the interest of escaping traditional historiography and its location within the modern epistemologies, base their representations on these subaltern theories, which are not developed as an alienating discursive practice but as a social practice that thinks *about* the present conditions of oppression, marginalization, and colonization *from* the perspective of those experiencing it as well as those resisting it.

In using this theorizing, subaltern histories turn out to be more than academic discourses; they constitute a social enterprise. They are not developed in isolation but in constant contact with the social situation and the subaltern's need for change. These counter-discourses are about offering a discursive space where the subaltern, who is constantly engaged in subversive experiences, finds a voice and a representation that opens the past to remembering. At the same time, subaltern histories need the subaltern and the subaltern's constant theorizing in order to be developed outside the centers of power that silence these voices in the first place. Both subversive practices, discursive and physical, are rooted in social justice and work together to achieve postcolonizing. As Dipesh Chakrabarty points out, "To wrench subaltern studies away from the keen sense of social justice that gave rise to the project would violate the spirit that gives this project its sense of commitment and intellectual energy."[54] Subaltern histories, then, in seeking social justice are also concerned with the construction of truth, not as a fixed category but as a process.

As I have suggested many times in this chapter, truth has always been a slippery term within history, and it is important to acknowledge that truth cannot be limited to the official knowledges. Truth, then, becomes a task, a process with an ethical perspective, because there is an ethical perspective in every epistemological concern. Not many historians acknowledge this ethical perspective as part of the historical task, but it seems to me that the process of truth is an ethical one. The historian needs an ethical commitment to the process. I believe, with Ketu H. Katrak, that "social responsibility must be

[53] Mignolo, *Local Histories*, 100 (emphasis in original).

[54] Chakrabarty, *Provincializing Europe*, 72.

the basis of any theorizing on postcolonial literature as well as the root of the creative work of the writers themselves."[55] This ethical standpoint invites historians to confront the modernist project and traditional historiography for their forms of exclusion, silencing, and oppression. This is what Enrique Dussel calls the ethics of liberation, that which "moves from the affirmation of the real, existent and historic other."[56] It is founded in personal relationships without domination or exploitation and in the "responsibility" for the subaltern, those who live in oppression and are real, not fictional characters of a novel.[57]

This ethical standpoint begins with self-critique. Scholars involved in postcolonizing criticism not only need to recognize the aspects explored above (i.e., traditional historiography as a colonial enterprise, the subjectivity and hybridity of the subaltern, the centrality of the subaltern's experiences within the construction of counter-discourses), but also need to acknowledge their own social location. In the same way, subaltern histories need to be self-critical about what they accomplish and what they do not, and historians need to be self-critical about their own biases and ideological perspectives. As Edward W. Said argues, "No one has ever devised a method for detaching the scholar from the circumstances of life, from the fact of his involvement (conscious or unconscious) with a class, a set of beliefs, a social position, or from the mere activity of being a member of a society."[58] However, committed scholars should be aware of their location in a particular circumstance of life, which is a privileged position, after all, while they have to choose to situate their work in the settings of those who suffer and live out oppression as well as struggle, resistance, and hope.

I understand many would argue that subaltern studies are passé, but because of their usefulness in dis-covering the voices of the

[55] Ketu H. Katrak, "Decolonizing Culture: Toward a Theory for Post-colonial Women's Texts," in Ashcroft, Griffiths, and Tiffin, *Post-colonial Studies Reader,* 255.

[56] Enrique Dussel, *Ética Comunitaria* (Madrid: Ediciones Paulinas, 1986), 262 (my translation).

[57] Dussel argues further, "El pobre, la clase oprimida, la nación periférica, la mujer objeto sexual, tienen realidad <<más allá>> del horizonte del sistema que los aliena, los reprime, los deshumaniza." Dussel, *Ética,* 262.

[58] Said, *Orientalism,* 10.

marginalized I still find them to be a viable approach. Latina/o religious history is in the process of constructing itself as a subaltern history, but I argue that it needs to organize itself in the context of postcolonizing criticism, as shown in this chapter, in order to practice the confrontation and dis-covery needed to achieve the reconstruction of the historical narratives. But, as I explored in the previous chapters, there are many methodological approaches that serve in the exploration of Latina/o religious history. Even further, as Chakrabarty argues, "In order to do this, historians concerned with recuperating peasant 'experience' in history have often turned to resources of other disciplines for help: anthropology, demography, sociology, archeology, human geography, etc."[59] In light of this, in the next two chapters I examine how two complementary methodological approaches, when employed through a postcolonizing approach, could be useful in the development of the field of Latina/o religious history as a subaltern history project.

[59] Chakrabarty, "Small History," 47. This fits perfectly with my point in the previous chapter about the sociological turn within U.S. Latina/o religious historiography.

6 LIVED RELIGION

Indeed, material culture offers a way of achieving the social historian's goal of expanding historical inquiry beyond great men and women to include ordinary people and everyday activities.

—Page Putnam Miller, "Landmarks of Women's History," in *Reclaiming the Past*, 9

Lived religion as an approach to the past and to the present opens up a rich array of possibilities for historians.

—David D. Hall, "Introduction," in *Lived Religion in America*, xi

Lived religion is constituted by the practices people use to remember, share, enact, adapt, create, and combine the stories out of which they live.

—Meredith B. McGuire, *Lived Religion*, 98

The subaltern, in order to offer resistance against colonial discourses, looks at different places to dis-cover their consciousness. The recuperation of this subaltern consciousness allows for the remembering of the past and the breaking of the normative understandings supported by those in power. Religious experiences become one of these spaces of resistance. The subaltern, through rituals and other religious practices that in most cases subvert the official religion, is able to connect a present condition to a hidden past. Thus, religious experiences say something about the history of the subaltern, and the question becomes how historians should examine these experiences in order to construct their narratives. Lived religion as a methodological approach is one of the answers to this question.

Lived religion refers to these religious practices of individuals and groups in everyday experiences. As sociologist Meredith B. McGuire argues, "The term 'lived religion' is useful for distinguishing the actual experience of religious persons from the prescribed religion of institutionally defined beliefs and practices."[1] As a historian, I can look at lived religions and be concerned about the reasons for these experiences or even the history of these practices, but I argue that from a postcolonizing perspective a historian explores the connections between these experiences and the past. As the subaltern is engaged in lived religion, she or he remembers, and thus the subaltern's consciousness is expanded. Here lies one of the historian's tasks in the construction of subaltern histories: to construct representations about the subaltern's past and how she or he is the subject of that development. Thus, historically, I take a deep analysis of lived religion into its connection to the subaltern's past.

In this sense the analysis of lived religion from a postcolonizing perspective is not merely a matter of looking at the history of rituals or religious practices within the context of the sacred. It is a matter of looking at these religious experiences within the particular context in which they are constructed, as it will vary as individuals and groups transform them from their own perspective and for their own benefit. In this chapter I examine lived religion as a useful methodological tool in the writing of subaltern histories. In the first section, I briefly look at the major aspects of lived religion and the way it has been developed as a theoretical approach. Examining the major concerns within this approach allows us to understand it and learn how it fits for subaltern histories. I then move on to explore how, through the injection of postcolonizing criticism, lived religion becomes a crucial approach in the study of Latina/o religious history.

LIVED RELIGION AS A METHODOLOGICAL APPROACH

Lived religion is born out of the sociological approach to the study of religion, especially as it pertains to the experiences of the people.

[1] Meredith B. McGuire, *Lived Religion: Faith and Practice in Everyday Life* (New York: Oxford University Press, 2008),

McGuire acknowledges that "this concept of religion is particularly apt for sociological analysis, because it depicts a subjectively grounded and potentially creative place for religious experience and expression."[2] In other words, this approach allows scholars to look at religion beyond its institutional baggage, and for historians it opens the door to the world of those who have been silenced by normative narratives. Traditionally, religious history is usually written as a narrative of what happens to a particular religious group or church in an organized, fixed way. "Historians have long represented religious leaders and followers like this, setting them within religious contexts in which everyone does what he or she is supposed to do, in which authority is obeyed and ritual rubrics carefully followed. Yet no one has ever seen anything like this in the real world."[3] A look at lived religion changes the possibilities of being able to create this type of narrative since it shows that the subaltern acts up against those in power, even through religious practices, which become places of transgressions against the established system.

Using lived religion, historians are able to examine religious experiences beyond their spiritual character and thus become cultural resources for individuals and/or communities in their everyday practices. In this sense lived religion is looking at the people's experiences within their context and not necessarily the result of an official tradition. Robert Orsi goes even further as he proposes that the use of lived religion "invite[s] a redirection of religious scholarship away from traditions—the great hypostatized constructs of 'Protestantism,' 'Catholicism,' and so on—and likewise away from denominational focus that has so preoccupied scholars of American religions, toward a study of how particular people, in particular places and times, live in, with, through, and against the religious idioms available to them in culture—*all* the idioms, including (often enough) those not explicitly their 'own.'"[4] People, and not institutions, are at the center of this approach. People's experiences are not hidden behind convention or even beliefs; they are explored as an important aspect of people's lives and, in many cases, as means of survival.

[2] McGuire, *Lived Religion*, 12.

[3] Robert Orsi, "Everyday Miracles: The Study of Lived Religion," in Hall, *Lived Religion in America*, 12.

[4] Orsi, "Everyday Miracles," 7 (emphasis in original).

WHY IS IT NECESSARY?

For ages, religion has been used as an instrument of colonization. Normative historical narratives have been concerned only with the perspective of the colonizer or the missionaries, and the experiences of the people have been marginalized as not important or less significant than those of the colonizer. People's religious experiences are left out from official and institutional religion. Looking at the official religion and its expressions does not allow us to see how people practice religion or what they actually take out of these practices. In other words, in the examination of the official religion, we find that the community does not occupy a central space within the narratives. There is no agency for the subaltern within these histories. In this case, it would seem as though religion is fixed and the practices have only one meaning, that which the colonizer imposed on them.

Lived religion is a matter of looking at religion from the perspective of the subaltern. In this case, lived religion is what others refer to as popular religion, which has been used by scholars to identify the religion of the people vis-à-vis the religion of the institution. This term is already filled with a tradition of ethnocentrism that sees the *popular* as marginal. Theologian Orlando O. Espín, in his description of how popular religion is viewed within academic settings, explains:

> Consequently, popular religion—to the degree that it is, indeed, a marginalized people's own—is insistently judged by theology and the social sciences as insufficient, superstitious, etc. At best, it is folklore—ultimately insignificant in the real world and to mainstream society. It is socially declared to be like its creators—of marginal interest.[5]

Further on in his discussion, Espín argues that it is important to redefine these understandings; it is in this popular religion that one can find "the real and unquestioned mainstream religion of U.S. Latinos."[6]

At the same time, other scholars, in order to encourage the use of the term lived religion over popular religion, argue that, since

[5] Orlando O. Espín, *The Faith of the People: Theological Reflections on Popular Catholicism* (Maryknoll, N.Y.: Orbis, 1997), 157.

[6] Espín, *Faith of the People*, 157.

the concept of popular religion is embedded with colonial nuances, it is better to use the term lived religion as a new understanding of these experiences comes to light and they acquire value. While in this book I prefer the use of the term lived religion, we should not dismiss the importance of the concept of popular religion because many scholars still use it as a way to challenge the fictional character of the universality of official religion. "The concept of popular religion has thus made it possible for historians to expand the scope of belief and practice beyond what was authorized by the institutional church."[7] In these *marginal* experiences, in popular religion, we not only find subversion of the tradition but also connections of the subaltern's consciousness to hidden pieces of the past.

Now, a danger lies in the interpretation of popular religion, or lived religion, as a tradition in itself, which would help essentialize the religious practices of the subaltern. This is why we need to address popular religion as heterogeneous, where the meaning is never fixed. "In popular religion, no authoritative voice exists that can establish what is the correct version of a popular tradition. As a result, the same popular tradition can serve to promote widely varying, even opposing social values."[8] The key is to study lived religion as oppositional knowledge, never static.

Lived religion is useful because it opens the discussion regarding the relationship between the subaltern and those in power. While the colonizer is always trying to impose colonial discourses, the subaltern finds ways of subverting the "official" through language, politics, art, and even religion. Lived religion serves the purpose of finding the ways that "popular religious expression still serves as a medium for expressing dissent from the larger society or resistance to an oppressive power, and popular culture can still express counterculture."[9] In other words, it is necessary to use lived religion as a methodological approach because it offers us a window to the hidden past through the subaltern's consciousness against the established narratives.

[7] Hall, "Introduction," viii.

[8] McGuire, *Lived Religion*, 53.

[9] McGuire, *Lived Religion*, 63.

HOW DOES IT WORK?

At first look, lived religion appears similar to the German-born historiographical approach called *Alltagsgeschichte,* or "history of everyday life." This approach focuses on the study of the daily lives (actions, work, thoughts, dreams, habits, etc.) of ordinary people. As Alf Lüdtke acknowledges:

> In doing history of everyday life, attention is focused not just on the deeds (and misdeeds) and pageantry of the great, the masters of church and state. Rather, central to the thrust of everyday historical analysis is the life and survival of those who have remained largely anonymous in history—the "nameless" multitudes in their workaday trials and tribulations, their occasional outbursts or *dépenses*.[10]

The subaltern in traditional historiography becomes visible as an actor in the history of everyday life. *Alltagsgeschichte* intends to establish that the subaltern is the subject in their life and that they respond to their context with agency. This is why context (social location, economics, religion, political location, gender, and other factors) turns out to be the key point in the history of everyday life. Accounts and actions cannot be alienated and studied apart from the context in which they took place.

In the same way, it is important to look at the subaltern's religious practices within their context, but not in a simplistic descriptive mode because we risk becoming reporters. This is one of the dangers within lived religion or history of everyday life, for that matter. While both focus on the representation of the subaltern as agent and subject, there is always a risk that the simple act of naming or mentioning the subaltern as important, without any in-depth analysis of her/his actions, especially as they challenge the dominant system, becomes the norm and is sufficient for many. I feel this is what seems to be happening in today's approach to history of the present: historians become journalists. In this sense, simplistic examinations prevent us from seeing that religious experiences are transformed from place to place, and by only offering descriptions

[10] Alf Lüdtke, "Introduction: What Is the History of Everyday Life and Who Are Its Practitioners?" in *The History of Everyday Life: Reconstructing Historical Experiences and Ways of Life,* ed. Alf Lüdtke, trans. William Templer (Princeton, N.J.: Princeton University Press, 1995), 3–4.

of them, we cause these practices to become fixed in time without gaining a deeper understanding of their meanings. Thus, religious experiences cannot be understood in a vacuum; we need a multiplicity of methodological approaches to study them.

While the use of sociological tools has been essential in this approach, historian David D. Hall argues that lived religion "is rooted less in sociology than in cultural and ethnographical approaches to the study of religion and American religious history that have come to the fore in recent years."[11] The use of cultural and ethnographical approaches implies that different methodologies are needed in lived religion. Because we are not dealing only with texts or places, but also with practices and interpretations, historians need to make use of a different methodology that in many cases, as Orsi finds, "is radically or phenomenologically empiricist, concerned with what people *do* with religious practice, what they make with it of themselves and their worlds."[12] It is a matter of using different methodologies from different perspectives in order not to reproduce the old traditional approaches but to redefine their use. Robert Orsi goes further in establishing the importance of avoiding fixed definitions on practices as he states that, "The key words here are tensile, hybridity, ambivalence, irony; the central methodological commitment is to avoid conclusions that impose univocality on practices that are multifarious."[13]

Ritual studies, cultural anthropological studies, congregational studies, oral histories, identity studies, and psychological and phenomenological analyses are among the many methodological approaches used to look at religious experiences as lived religion. Through these approaches the historian is able to examine everyday experiences within their context, because within lived religion it is important to analyze every aspect that affects the experience (e.g., culture, language, location). Once one takes these aspects into consideration, it is easy to see the subaltern's religious experiences as hybrid and in constant development. This is why, as Hall hints, no matter what methodology is used, some ethnographical work is involved because it is the way to look at actual practices through the eyes of those subjects.

[11] Hall, "Introduction," vii.

[12] Orsi, "Everyday Miracles," 7 (emphasis in original).

[13] Orsi, "Everyday Miracles," 11.

In many cases, historians who use lived religion in their work follow more than one methodological approach in order to get an extensive understanding of religious experiences. For example, Arlene M. Sánchez Walsh uses oral histories, congregational histories, and ethnographical observation as part of her work on Latina/o Pentecostals. Thomas A. Tweed and Timothy Matovina use ritual studies, material culture analysis, identity analysis, and ethnographical observation, among others, in their respective works on the Cuban community in Miami and the devotion to Our Lady of Charity, and the Mexican-American community in San Antonio and the devotion to Our Lady of Guadalupe.[14] Within studies of lived religion, these methodological approaches work together to prevent these experiences from being explored in a vacuum.

WHAT DO WE GET?

Because of the use of different methodological approaches in case studies, there is no one particular way of putting historical narratives together following lived religion analysis. Even further, since religious experiences are not confined to modern understandings, it is hard to translate religious experiences into academic discourses because there are limits to the meanings these experiences can provide us. For the most part, scholars involved in lived religion have focused on exploring these experiences, their histories, and how individuals and communities partake of them. They read these experiences as part of a cultural context and construct them as academic discourses in organized narratives. Of course, there is always the danger of essentializing them and fixing them into coherent narratives, which popular religions are not. The result of this difficult task is the introduction of the religious practices of the people as being outside the official religion. The value of these is assigned by each scholar's particular interpretation of the experiences in light of the context.

[14] Arlene M. Sánchez Walsh, *Latino Pentecostal Identity: Evangelical Faith, Self, and Society* (New York: Columbia University Press, 2003); Timothy Matovina, *Guadalupe and Her Faithful: Latino Catholics in San Antonio, from Colonial Origins to the Present* (Baltimore: Johns Hopkins University Press, 2005); and Thomas A. Tweed, *Our Lady of the Exile: Diasporic Religion at a Cuban Catholic Shrine in Miami* (New York: Oxford University Press, 1997).

For example, theologically, from a liberationist perspective, an analysis of these experiences may show that religion can work as a source of liberation for those who practice popular religion in order to subvert the official religion. Sociologically, this type of analysis may show that a group finds comfort and meaning in the celebration of religious practices in light of their sociopolitical marginalization. I find that historically, this type of analysis may show the development of an individual's religious experience and/or a community's religious experience. As I have mentioned before, the challenge is to acquire meaning beyond the descriptive aspect that historians usually settle for. I am not devaluing the importance of the descriptive character of these historical narratives. These descriptions are essential in the elucidation of the ways the subaltern subverts tradition through religious experiences. But I believe that a deeper analysis can provide a better understanding not only of the religious development but also of the development of the community. Thus it is important that the analysis of these religious experiences include a postcolonizing perspective, which allows not only for the representation of the dis-covered practices but also provides a challenge to the traditional discourses that have hidden these experiences in the first place.

POSTCOLONIZING LIVED RELIGION

In order to use postcolonizing criticism within the study of lived religion, it is important first to recognize that religious experiences are not just about experiences of God within culture but represent subversive actions. Traditional discourses, which may have been constructed by religious institutions or traditions, are responsible for the subaltern not being able to see her/his culture represented within the official religion. Lived religion breaks these constructions so the subaltern reinterprets her/his identity through the dis-covery of a consciousness. I am not referring to a simple religious consciousness that situates the subaltern within a religious past, but to a historical consciousness that reinforces a cultural memory and the presence of cultural identities among the subaltern, identities that are outside the colonial discourses of representations promoted by those in power. Through religious experiences, then, the subaltern is able to remember, and to connect its present to pieces of the past in order to recreate cultural identities.

As historians, our task within the postcolonizing perspective is to examine these practices and the way they connect to the hidden past in order to construct representations of those pieces of the past without essentializing them as *the* history. These representations need to be grounded in the context of the subaltern and to focus on the way these subjective activities break the traditional discourses as subversive experiences. Now, in our representations we need to be careful about presenting these experiences as fixed symbols of the new narratives with only one meaning. Historian Robert Orsi urges that a new way of looking at historiography is needed in this case:

> If appropriated and inherited religious idioms do not reflect or mirror the world but make it, then a historiography is required that does not look for religious windows onto wider social or cultural realities and does not treat religious creations as icons of history, but instead seeks to understand religious idioms dynamically, in place. The questions with which we approach religion should not concern frozen "meanings" but should instead query the complexities of lived religious practices.[15]

Through a postcolonizing perspective we can fulfill this call for a new historiography that grasps the complexities of meanings, and offers representations without overarching universal conclusions. Our approach to lived religion, then, needs to be founded on openness of discourse. By openness I mean the creation of discourses that are self-critical and specific about the ideology behind the interpretations of the author. For example, within postcolonizing criticism the religious experiences of the subaltern are seen as places of transgression against those in power. That is a reading of these experiences, and in no way does a reading define the *reality* of these activities. This recognition needs to be present in order not to advance the idea that one approach is the only one, or that one reading of the situation encompasses everything. Thus, let me focus on two issues I believe are essential for scholars in the construction of historical narratives on lived religion from a postcolonizing perspective: the role of the researcher/author, and the subversive character of the task.

[15] Orsi, "Everyday Miracles," 10.

ROLE OF THE RESEARCHER/AUTHOR

There is no *one* particular way to analyze lived religion. On the contrary, because of the multiplicity of methodological approaches that could be used in this task, the analysis will depend on the tools available to the historian. The analysis needs to take into consideration the research aspects of the project and the way the historian will interpret and translate the data into a historical discourse. Within a postcolonizing perspective, the creation of the research agenda needs to include self-critical assertions regarding the social location of the researcher. Some may leave this task to the end as they analyze the way the discourse was constructed, but here I argue that if a postcolonizing criticism is going to be followed, this needs to be one of the first things to do: locate oneself in regard to the subjects of study. This allows the historian to distinguish the ideology, purpose, and possible sought outcome behind her/his interest in the particular project. Because ethnographical work is important in the study of lived religion, these three aspects will influence the kind of observations, questioning, and/or interaction the historian will have in the research. In other words, this kind of self-evaluation helps explain the role of the historian as a researcher and author within the project.

The role of the researcher is especially important within ethnographic work because it not only affects the way one evaluates what is observed, but also the way the subjects act when a researcher is participating in religious experiences. Dipesh Chakrabarty identifies this challenging task for the researcher as he states, "Ethnographic observation, similarly, is based on the ethnographer himself or herself shuttling between the two distinct roles of the participant and the observer, but here also analysis entails the conversion of the participant's involved and engaged eye into the distant and disinterested eye of the observer."[16] Chakrabarty focuses on the idea that the researcher, by participating in the historical event, will have trouble adjusting the type of observation she/he is doing. I argue that if the researcher was able to be self-critical before the project began, she/he would avoid this predicament of being either participant or observer because she/he would have already accepted her/his own subjectivity.

[16] Dipesh Chakrabarty, *Provincializing Europe: Postcolonial Thought and Historical Difference* (Princeton, N.J.: Princeton University Press, 2000), 239.

Even further, I agree with cultural anthropologist Kirin Narayan on the need to look beyond the "dichotomy between outsider/insider or observer/observed" when looking at the role of anthropologists.[17] She proposes that "at this historical moment we might more profitably view each anthropologist in terms of shifting identifications amid a field of interpenetrating communities and power relations."[18] Thus, the researcher needs to understand her/his positioning within these complex relationships with the subjects. Narayan explains the importance of looking at this relation as it pertains to the subjects:

> Instead, what we must focus our attention on is the quality of relations with the people we seek to represent in our texts: are they viewed as mere fodder for professionally self-serving statements about a generalized Other, or are they accepted as subjects with voices, views, and dilemmas—people to whom we are bonded through ties of reciprocity and who may even be critical of our professional enterprise?[19]

The location of the subjects within our narratives can only be explained by our own sociocultural location and perspective. The task of the historian within a postcolonizing perspective is to be open and self-critical about that positioning.

This positioning is essential because within modern thought the idea of objectivity is a central characteristic of superior discourse. Following this modernist perspective it would be possible for the researcher to be stripped of her/his *essence* in order to grasp the historical events from an unbiased perch of observation. Chakrabarty explains this angle as he writes:

> If historical or anthropological consciousness is seen as the work of a rational outlook, it can only "objectify"—and thus deny—the *lived* relations the observing subject already has with that which he or she identifies as belonging to a historical or ethnographic time and space separate from the ones he or she occupies as the

[17] Kirin Narayan, "How Native Is a 'Native' Anthropologist?" in *Feminist Postcolonial Theory: A Reader,* ed. Reina Lewis and Sara Mills (New York: Routledge, 2003), 285. As scholars engage in ethnographical work, historians act as anthropologists, and, thus, my use of Narayan's perspective.

[18] Narayan, "How Native," 285.

[19] Narayan, "How Native," 286.

> analyst. In other words, the method does not allow the investigating subject to recognize himself or herself as also the figure he or she is investigating. It stops the subject from seeing his or her own present as discontinuous with itself.[20]

Postcolonizing criticism exposes this objectivity as a false construct that is unachievable because every individual is a social being, filled with biases and perspectives that inform her/his actions.[21] As Narayan explains, "'Objectivity' must be replaced by an involvement that is unabashedly subjective as it interacts with and invites other subjectivities to take a place in anthropological productions."[22] This recognition of subjectivity allows historians to acknowledge both that they do not come to the research without some knowledge of or relationship with the people and that those perceptions can change through fieldwork.[23]

Now, this subjectivity (ideology, bias, etc.) should be clearly introduced in the narrative. Historian Hayden White argues that the ethical elements in the historian's assumptions are reflected in the ideological dimensions of her/his historical account.[24] Through the introduction of a particular ideological agenda and methodological scaffolds within the body of the project, historians can understand the particularity and limits of their work. They will be engaged in the task of truth, understanding that they will never fully grasp the truth, only work toward it. Historians who recognize the power/knowledge relationship within their own work and introduce their biases, exclusions, and silences at the beginning of the project will acknowledge the absence of any kind of universality within or produced by their discourses. The authors have control over their projects, and in this sense this postmodern view does not take away

[20] Chakrabarty, *Provincializing Europe*, 239 (emphasis in original).

[21] Since modern thought is embedded within academic settings, I recognize the danger of admitting subjectivity within one's research, as it may be categorized as "contextual" or "popular," idioms that suggest marginal or second-grade knowledge. But if the researcher follows the postcolonizing project, traditional historical narratives are exposed as subjective since they are written from a particular perspective and for the benefit of those in power.

[22] Narayan, "How Native," 300.

[23] Narayan, "How Native," 295.

[24] Hayden White, *Metahistory: The Historical Imagination in Nineteenth-Century Europe* (Baltimore: Johns Hopkins University Press, 1973), 22.

the control of the individual. In this sense, the authors are still the agents of construction, and they do not lose their subjectivity. As Joan Wallach Scott argues,

> Such a reflexive, self-critical approach makes apparent the particularistic status of any historical knowledge and the historian's active role as a producer of knowledge. It undermines claims for authority based on totalizing explanations, essentialized categories of analysis (be they human nature, race, class, sex, or "the oppressed"), or synthetic narratives that assume an inherent unity for the past.[25]

Because within Latina/o religious history most historians are part of the communities they explore, at least tangentially, there is a danger that as authors we may assume our subjectivity is founded within our subjects, without understanding the distance between the two. Narayan discusses this problem while also offering us a solution:

> To highlight the personal and intellectual dilemmas invoked by the assumption that a "native" anthropologist can represent an unproblematic and authentic insider's perspective, I incorporate personal narrative into a wider discussion of anthropological scholarship. Tacking between situated narrative and more sweeping analysis, I argue for the *enactment of hybridity* in our texts; that is, writing that depicts authors as minimally bicultural in terms of belonging simultaneously to the world of engaged scholarship and the world of everyday life.[26]

Enacting this hybridity allows those of us who are Latina/o historians to see ourselves within our multiple locations without pretending that we are just participants observing from within, or that we are able to compartmentalize our personal experiences and separate them from our academic work. Our subjectivity gets exposed while our discourses are not constructed without the fictional imaginary of universality. The knowledge within them "is not transcendental,

[25] Joan Wallach Scott, *Gender and the Politics of History* (New York: Columbia University Press, 1999), 7–8.

[26] Narayan, "How Native," 286 (emphasis in original).

but situated, negotiated and part of an ongoing process," that "spans personal, professional and cultural domains."[27]

The question, then, becomes what type of approach should be used to produce these historical representations now that the objectivity of historical discourses has been debunked. Historians have been using emplotment as a way to construct narratives that follow a linear perspective, where each aspect and event fits within an order. In this sense, narrative writing became the preferred mode of communication by historians and they sought to hide behind it as if the past itself were constructed in narrative form. In the past, I have argued that it would be difficult to do away with narrative as a means of communication within historiography, but that narratives should "become self-critical and self-referential discourses, rather than conveyers of universal truths."[28] Once the role of the researcher/author is exposed and acknowledged, historical narrativizing would also be transformed. Thus, as in subaltern histories, in the process of narrativizing about lived religion, historians need to understand that "narratives are not transparent representations of what actually happened, but told for particular purposes, from particular points of view: they are thus incipiently analytical, enacting theory."[29] The subaltern is given space to speak about these religious experiences within the narratives, as the creation of narrative should not be simply a descriptive process controlled by the author. At the same, the author, understanding her/his subjectivity, provides context, analysis, and interpretation. Within postcolonizing criticism, the research and this twofold process of writing historical discourses should be, then, understood as a subversive practice.

SUBVERSION AND TRANSGRESSION

In order to confront the normative knowledges and dis-cover new representations from the perspective of the subaltern, historians need to acknowledge their task as a process of transgression. Not

[27] Narayan, "How Native," 300.

[28] Hjamil A. Martínez-Vázquez, "Breaking the Established Scaffold: Imagination as a Resource in the Development of Biblical Interpretation," in *Her Master's Tools? Feminist and Post-colonial Engagements of Historical-Critical Discourse*, SBL Global Perspectives on the Bible 9, ed. Todd Penner and Caroline Vander Stichele (Atlanta: Society of Biblical Literature, 2005), 82.

[29] Narayan, "How Native," 299.

only are the modernist perspectives deconstructed, as explained above, but also analysis and interpretation need to focus on the representation of these religious activities as subversive actions. Historians transgress the normative historical narratives to prove the way these subaltern experiences break them apart and show their discontinuities. Historians are able to participate in this transgression by focusing on the subaltern not as an artifact of history, whose activities are celebrated and *fixed* within museums as if they represent authenticity of the subaltern, but as an active participant in the continuous process of construction and reconstruction of cultural identities.[30]

This postcolonizing call for subversion and transgression is my response to the danger of becoming fascinated with the subaltern as a relic that is *exhibited* within a discourse and *it* acquires meaning that way. I refer to this approach as museum historical education, in which an object or activity from a particular community is shown in a museum and the visitor is able not only to *know everything* about that artifact or activity but also about the community. For example, in an exhibition about Mexican-American culture, one is almost bound to find some skull images or altars in reference to the celebration of the Day of the Dead. The visitor, who does not understand the complexities of this celebration or the multiplicity of understandings of it, believes that the representation (artifact) explains everything about it. Historical discourses about the subaltern tend to follow this approach as the subaltern is romanticized.[31] These narratives are constructed through a descriptive approach in which the subaltern is not a subject, and the experiences are viewed as practices without particular values assigned to them. For example, songs, rituals, and special prayers are described as part of the experience,

[30] For more information about the way representations of the subaltern can become "myth-making" artifacts of authenticity, see Rey Chow, "Where Have All the Natives Gone?" in Reina and Mills, *Feminist Postcolonial Theory,* 324–49.

[31] Even within my own representations here, I run the danger of romanticizing the subaltern as always subversive when it is clear that not all subaltern activities are subversive. The difference is that within a postcolonizing approach, my discourse is just one discourse that follows my own political ideology and in no way fixes the subaltern into one category. In other words, my discourse is a representation following my own observations through particular lenses, not a definition of the subaltern.

but they are not explored as important actions of the subaltern. Through postcolonizing criticism, lived religion is an approach that not only dis-covers these songs, rituals, and prayers, but also examines the way these represent, or do not represent, subversive activities that generate cultural memory. In other words, these narratives do not simply represent photographs of religious experiences.

Hence, it is not sufficient to dis-cover and describe these religious experiences. It is important to understand them beyond their religious significance. Many works within lived religion do an excellent job of examining the experiences within their particular context and in some cases even as they confront the official religious traditions. But I argue that in order to fully grasp the multiple meanings of these experiences, it is important to see them as cultural acts of subversion and remembering. For the historian, it is important, then, to approach religious experiences as a way in which the subaltern makes theory through praxis.

In the case of Latina/o religious history, this analysis of theory as praxis is essential because many of the activities of Latina/o religious communities take place outside the church, or at least outside the "contours" of institutional power. This praxis does not simply go against the official religion, but also goes against the whole traditional system of knowledge. Thus, praxis acquires a subversive quality. Challenging the official religion is important, as it pokes holes in the tradition, but challenging the normative knowledges opens the door to the dismantling of the colonial discourses. Locating these religious experiences within the realm of the subaltern's acts of transgression reveals the way religious experiences can be used as a source of liberation, not just in the physical domain but also in the discursive arena. Our discourses need to reflect these transgressions as we confront the traditional historical narratives.

Postcolonizing injects a clear and obvious sense of subversion into our analysis, not simply to expose but to deconstruct. At the center of this task is the subaltern. Through ethnographical work, interviews, analysis of experiences, and reinterpretation of the past (a past that has been found as discontinuous), we are able to see and represent how the subaltern, through the act of remembering, is able find pieces of the past that allow for the reconstruction of cultural identities. At the same time, this remembering destroys the normative knowledges that have been fixed. We need to expose this as part of our discourses. Thus, the political aspect of our task needs to be front and center as we reconstruct the representations of the subaltern.

For example, in the case of Latina/o religious history, postcolonizing criticism, with its subjective and political agenda, illustrates the way lived religion, such as the devotion to Our Lady of Charity in Miami and Our Lady of Guadalupe in San Antonio, beyond offering new insights on these two communities and their subversion against the institution and the official religion, offers a challenge to the traditional historical narratives. Even further, the subaltern's capacity to remember some pieces of the past through rituals dismantles the normative perception of Latinas/os as recipients of religion through colonization or missionary enterprise. In the same way, an analysis of Afro-Caribbean religious experiences among Latinas/os also goes beyond the establishment of these communities to a multi-layered past, tearing down the false constructs within religious historical discourses by opening the door to new religious systems that have been hidden. Since historians do not have an easy task in the production of representations of these pieces of the past, remembered by the subaltern through religious experiences, I am just offering suggestions on how to become intentional in our task of subversion.

These religious experiences should be seen from a postcolonizing perspective as acts of resistance through practice. Orsi establishes that lived religion as a place of resistance "emphasizes dissent, subversion, and resistance, rather than harmony, consensus, and social legitimation."[32] In these acts of dissent, the subaltern is able not only to step away from the official religion through popular expressions of religion, but also to construct counter-discourses through practices that offer opposition to the discourses of oppression and fixed identity. The latter aspect of opposition is what postcolonizing criticism is interested in exploring further, because as the subaltern perceives these rituals as a source of cultural memory she/he is able to see beyond the historical consciousness imposed by tradition. This subaltern historical consciousness is concerned with the past, but only as it is informed with the present condition of the subaltern. Thus, the past is not fixed but interpreted, remembered. The past acquires vitality in the religious experiences of the subaltern, because it is not dead or fixed in a distant period of time but alive in those practices. Through these practices the subaltern accesses those discontinuities

[32] Orsi, "Everyday Miracles," 15.

in official history that I mentioned in the previous chapter, as it is in these spaces that pieces of the past that have been hidden (or erased) are found.

Let me explore further the role of memory in this process. The subaltern accesses pieces of the past through that cultural memory exposed within religious experiences. Memory is the link to that historical consciousness that is being dis-covered as the subaltern remembers. Cultural memory becomes, in this sense, part of the subversive activity because it allows for the dis-covery of that consciousness, outside the traditional discourses. It is this consciousness that transgresses against the colonial historical narratives. Memory works to reach those hidden spaces of the past, not because they can be brought as if they were objects to recover, but because in the reconstruction of them, the subaltern finds new perspectives and stories that inform the reconstruction of cultural identities.[33] Thus, not only are the discontinuities of the past exposed, but this new approach also breaks the false impression that historical discourses are continuous and follow a linear development. On the contrary, subaltern histories understand that the process of *representing* a complex past is never structured in a linear way.

Now, before continuing it is important to clarify an important point. Religious experiences do not only impact the life of the subaltern; those in power also experience religion in their everyday life. The difference is that when those in power experience religion, they simply live out experiences that connect to a fixed past, so no remembering is needed because they are able to see themselves in that past. These practices speak about what has made it through the filter of traditional history. The subaltern has not made it through that filter of history and so cannot see herself/himself within these practices, and decides to create new ones that break through that

[33] Some may argue that this is the difference between subaltern histories and *real* history: subaltern histories are constructed on the basis of the need of the subaltern and not on truth, as are dominant historical discourses. While a comprehensive discussion on the nature of the truth gathered by historical narratives lies beyond the scope of this work, it is important to acknowledge that contrary to this misleading argument, I argue that all history is written from someone's perspective and for someone's gain, and that those in power generally have been the ones to write the dominant narrative representations of history. As representations, these narratives are not truth but interpretations of the past based on ideologies and cultural contexts.

filter, exposing pieces of the subaltern's hidden past. "People can create new popular practices, adapt old ones, and ignore those traditions that are not meaningful or useful in their lives."[34] The subaltern is able to develop religious practices and rituals that allow the dis-covery of a cultural memory. Once the subaltern acquires this cultural memory, she/he is able to contest the meanings of traditional religious practices and to begin the process of constructing cultural identities, which are never fixed and are always recreating themselves with the constant cultural changes.

The task of subversion not only undermines the colonial discourses supported by those in power, but also undermines many of the subaltern's own processes of self-identification, which lead to the mistaken idea of the existence of a particular single subaltern identity. These erroneous calls for sameness are founded on the need to create an identity different from those in power in order to establish some challenge to the dominant culture. The problem is that these exercises of resistance reproduce the dualistic attitude (us vs. them) proposed by the modern system and supported by those in power. Dualism produces the essentialization of both groups, where their identities are defined and fixed. McGuire finds that within the construction of group identities, it is highly probable that these constructions of boundaries happen. She writes:

> This representation of the solidarity of such a group as a natural bond not only protects the group's legitimating myth's foundations from being questioned but also gives that myth the potential to reify and essentialize group identity. The myth legitimates group identity and solidarity, affirming: This is who we naturally—in our essence—are and always have been. And the myth legitimates oppositional boundaries toward the Other, whose identity is likewise constructed as historically fixed and essential. The idea of a pure and unitary tradition, uninfluenced by any cultural hybridity, is closed connected with this kind of legitimating myth.[35]

From a postcolonizing perspective, lived religion as a subversive practice contests the existence of this dualism. Because of their openness to constant difference and hybridity, subaltern cultural

[34] McGuire, *Lived Religion*, 60–61.
[35] McGuire, *Lived Religion*, 207.

identities are unfinished products. It is this constant development and hybrid aspect that actually separates these identities from the fixed representations of the colonial discourses that do not value heterogeneity. Even when dominant identities are also hybrid, not pure, they get essentialized all the same, and thus difference is only used as it pertains to the construction of the Other.

Lived religion as a theoretical approach, within postcolonizing criticism, is aware of these multiple transgressions by the subaltern while at the same time taking into consideration the constant hybridization of identities. Thus, the task is not as simple as understanding the past in light of the present. One has to examine the heterogeneous contexts that conform these developments. People do not practice or experience religion in the same way. On the contrary, rituals and other religious practices have gone through many developmental changes as the social context of the subaltern also has changed and they have accessed pieces of the past. These constant transformations show proof of the agency of the subaltern, who is not dependent upon tradition. The subaltern generates religious practices that not only "make sense" but also allow the further development of a historical consciousness.

7 FEMINIST HISTORY

Feminism, as a methodological tool, would unleash systems of thought from restrictive categories, the categories of modernity in which Chicana history had been trapped. However, although historians of women questioned traditional history that excluded women, excluded the way gender carved history, women of color historians questioned how feminism, too, had its flaws.

—Emma Pérez, *The Decolonial Imaginary*, 22

We Chicanas, along with other previously unlistened-to subaltern women, now insist on our agency to speak for ourselves. The question remains—who will listen and how well equipped with relevant information is that audience?

—Sonia Saldívar-Hull, *Feminism on the Border*, 55

In her essay "Women and Religion," Jean R. Soderlund acknowledges that, "While women comprised the majority of the faithful in many denominations, they lacked access to leadership and authority."[1] This has also been the case for Latinas within their religious communities, and that lack of leadership has prevented them from trying to break away from this reality of marginalization. In this regard, historian Lara Medina explains:

[1] Jean R. Soderlund, "Women and Religion," in *Reclaiming the Past: Landmarks of Women's History*, ed. Page Putnam Miller (Bloomington: Indiana University Press, 1992), 176.

> Although many Latinas participate in patriarchal religions that attempt a male monopoly over the sacred, Latinas carry on with their own understandings of the sacred and have oftentimes carved autonomous spaces for women within these religions. Other Latinas engage in religions such as santeria, where women maintain priestly leadership status; curanderismo, where *el don*, or the gift of healing, enables women to transcend gender constructions; or Indigenous spiritual paths that are traditionally egalitarian.[2]

But even with the creation of these spaces of leadership, the experiences of Latinas, as historical subjects, were left out of many historical narratives about Latina/o religions. While the development and incorporation of feminist approaches to historical writing have challenged traditional perspectives within the larger field of history, there is still much work to be done within Latina/o religious historiography. In this chapter, I explore the way feminist methodological approaches would advance the construction of Latina/o religious histories as subaltern histories. Thus, I am not arguing that feminist criticism only serves in the recuperation of Latinas as subjects, but that this kind of approach functions to improve the whole field.

For example, as mentioned before and as Medina finds, "The Eurocentric biases of the 'official' church led to the marginalization of 'popular' Mexican Catholic traditions with their rich pageantry and women-centered rituals practiced by the working class."[3] Since most of the women's activities are categorized as "popular," they are marginalized and left out of the traditional historical narratives. As part of the lived religion of the Latina/o community, the examination of these activities becomes essential in the recuperation of the Latina/o subaltern past in order to construct new historical representations. A feminist approach that works within postcolonizing criticism would only increase the possibility of dis-covering the voices of the subaltern as they are engaged in subversive activities through religious experiences.

This chapter is divided into two major sections. In the first part, I briefly examine the development of the field of feminist history.

[2] Lara Medina, "Women: The U.S. Latina Religious Experience," in *Introduction to the U.S. Latina and Latino Religious Experience*, ed. Hector Avalos (Boston: Brill Academic, 2004), 284–85.

[3] Medina, "Women," 290–91.

This study allows us to recognize the movement from women's history to feminist history, and the inclusion of gender as a category of analysis. Then, I proceed to discuss the specific use of feminist criticism within the study of the Latina/o community in order to explore the ways this could be useful in the writing of Latina/o religious history. As in the previous chapter, my analysis here serves to continue to offer options about how to use postcolonizing criticism in this historical field.

FROM WOMEN'S HISTORY TO FEMINIST HISTORY

Women's history, and the latter construction of feminist history, has emerged as one of the most important fields in the academy. Joan Wallach Scott, one of the leading theorists in the field, has argued that there have been three stages in the development of this field: 1) a direct connection with politics, 2) a separation from politics, and 3) introducing the category of gender into the discussion.[4] The first stage was characterized by a constant searching for the agency and presence of women in history, and the exposition of oppression, which led to resistance. The second involved a step away from politics to include not only the social actions of women, but also their internal struggles and points of view. Finally, the introduction of the concept of gender "was a definitive break with politics and so enabled this field to come into its own, for gender is a seemingly neutral term devoid of immediate ideological purpose."[5] Scott finds that these stages represent a movement "from feminism to women to gender; that is from politics to specialized history to analysis."[6] While I do not disagree with Scott's analysis, let me explore further this development and its characteristics and theoretical frameworks.

Without a doubt, the absence of women as subjects in historical narratives provoked the development of studies in the area. Historians, mostly women, began to uncover the faces, names, facts, and situations of many women. Women's stories were exposed, but as Page Putnam Miller acknowledges, "Women's history began with an emphasis on compensatory history, to bring to light women's

[4] Joan Wallach Scott, "Women's History," in *New Perspectives in Historical Writing*, ed. Peter Burke (University Park: Pennsylvania State University Press, 1991), 42–66.

[5] Scott, "Women's History," 43.

[6] Scott, "Women's History," 43.

contributions to American society."[7] It was after this that there was a movement from this compensatory phase to the inclusion of deeper analysis, in which "the effort goes far beyond the naïve search for the heroic ancestors of the contemporary women's movement to a reevaluation of established standards of historical significance."[8] At this time, the inclusion of these names became more than a supplement or footnote to the traditional narrative; it became a new way of doing history. Alan Munslow acknowledges, "No doubt including women in history forced historians to confront not just what has hitherto been missing in history by adding women and women's experience, but this move must entail the second meaning of supplement, a substitution for what presently exists."[9] In order words, this approach was not just about including names, stories, and places in the traditional narrative, but entailed a challenge to the traditional historical paradigms in order to perform a constructive critique to the field of history.

Women's history, as proposed by Scott, goes further into the analysis of the meanings within texts. Following a poststructuralist approach, she started questioning the notions of modern epistemology, especially those related to the essentialized character of gender relations. Women were introduced into traditional history with a particular definition, arguing that through history the notion of what a woman is turns out to be the same. The way to deconstruct this paradigm is to challenge the language of the discourse, a language based on male dominance. It is in language that the construction of meaning takes place, so man, using *his*tory, defined himself as opposition to the Other. The Other, including women, non-whites, and non-Westerners, was defined in the language of man, in his own terms and by his own power. In this sense, women were defined in a peculiar way. The deconstruction of meanings, then, leads to the liberation of women's categories from male dominance. This project does not merely challenge ideology, politics, or ethics, but goes on to confront modern epistemology directly. "The heart of

[7] Page Putnam Miller, "Landmarks of Women's History," in Miller, *Reclaiming the Past*, 8.

[8] Joan Wallach Scott, *Gender and the Politics of History* (New York: Columbia University Press, 1999), 17.

[9] Alan Munslow, *The Routledge Companion to Historical Studies* (London: Routledge, 2000), 228.

the epistemological challenge to proper history posed by women's history converges, therefore, on the conceptualization of difference construed and constituted through the cultural construction of meaning and knowledge, and the power of language."[10] Of course, not all women historians have followed this postmodern approach, since many still follow empiricism and the ultimate quest for truth. They have challenged the content and direction of the narrative with the inclusion of the categories of women and gender, but they have not disputed the scaffold that holds traditional historiography together.

The postmodern feminist approach to history, which turns out to be in many senses a subversive enterprise, maintains that the present historical landscape has not changed and that it is still controlled by modern epistemology. By analyzing established assumptions and practices, such as the universality of its content, women's history exposes the relationship of power—subordination and domination—within the construction of knowledge. But in order to really reveal these structures of power and challenge them, history's positivism has to be left behind. Again, Scott argues that this positivist paradigm has expanded the topics of history and has included women, "but writing about women as, say, workers or members of the working class did not effectively change established definitions of those categories, nor did it shed light on why those writing labor history had ignored evidence about women for so long."[11] In other words, it does not challenge the way history is written; it only adds voices and names to the narrative. She insists on the need for a "more radical epistemology" based on poststructuralism, which asks the question of *how* meanings are constructed. "The emphasis on 'how' suggests a study of process, not of origins, of multiple rather than single causes, of rhetoric or discourse rather than ideology or consciousness."[12]

This shift toward theory allows women's history to work on the scrutiny of the past while, at the same time, it tries to change the reality of subordination and oppression. It is a political project, and cannot be disregarded as a nihilistic process as other deconstructionist approaches have been. By analyzing the construction of meanings in history through language, especially constructions about gender,

[10] Munslow, *Routledge Companion*, 229.

[11] Scott, *Gender and the Politics*, 3.

[12] Scott, *Gender and the Politics*, 4.

this postmodern perspective "permits the kind of critical assessment of their discipline that feminist historians need in order to pursue their goal of making women historical subjects."[13] Traditional history participates, supports, and perpetuates the production of gender knowledge, and, as Scott acknowledges, the theoretical tool of examination "offers a way to generate new knowledge about women and sexual difference *and* to inspire critical challenges to the politics of history, or for that matter, any other discipline."[14] Thus, as mentioned above, women's history involves more than a mere supplement to traditional history. It critically deconstructs the discipline as a site for the construction of gender knowledge. By following this political and theoretical project, there is a move from women's history to feminist history.

But, even with the movement toward a more political and theoretical approach, Western feminist history began to work as a hegemonic approach. While gender, as a hermeneutical tool, did indeed open the field to a broader analysis of historiography, Western feminist history was unable to include issues of race or class within their analysis. Sonia Saldívar-Hull describes the effect of this decision:

> When the leading European and Anglo-American feminists working in the 1970s and the 1980s displaced, misplaced, or outright ignored Chicana feminisms and other feminisms articulated by U.S. women of color, they inadvertently colonized the very terms *feminism* and *politics*. The strategies of containment practiced against feminists of color include a feminist theory that does not recognize race as a component of women's identity.[15]

This means that the representations of women were based on white women's experiences. In response to that event, women of color began to redefine feminism and women's liberation in order actually to incorporate race and class within the analysis, acknowledging the importance of context in the examination of women's lives. To that effect, bell hooks explains that, "Women in lower-class and poor groups, particularly those who are non-white, would not have defined women's liberation as women gaining social equality with

[13] Scott, *Gender and the Politics*, 9.

[14] Scott, *Gender and the Politics*, 10 (emphasis in original).

[15] Sonia Saldívar-Hull, *Feminism on the Border: Chicana Gender Politics and Literature* (Berkeley: University of California Press, 2000), 39.

men, since they are continually reminded in their everyday lives that all women do not share a common social status."[16] Women of color confronted Western feminism for its representation of women of color as monolithic and its failure to make connections to other modes of resistance.

Chela Sandoval, in her discussions about oppositional consciousness, recognizes that while forms of feminisms within the dominant groups of society do indeed represent opposition, "Hegemonic feminism appears incapable of making the connections between its own expressions of resistance and opposition and the expressions of consciousness in opposition enacted amongst other racial, ethnic, cultural or gender liberation movements."[17] She finds that U.S. third-world feminism provides not only an oppositional consciousness but also a "differential" mode of consciousness that does not follow the traditional topography of hegemonic feminism. This differential consciousness challenges traditional modes of representation of women even when they come from hegemonic feminism. As Sandoval acknowledges, "U.S. third-world feminism represents a central locus of possibility, an insurgent movement which shatters the construction of any one of the collective ideologies as the single most correct site where truth can be represented."[18] It represents a new way of looking at subjectivity, "a political revision that denies any one ideology as the final answer, while instead positing a *tactical subjectivity* with the capacity to recenter depending upon the kinds of oppression to be confronted."[19] Emma Pérez also describes this theory of differential consciousness as the space where one can find "the decolonizing subject negotiating new histories."[20] In light of this, I argue that Latina/o religious histories from a feminist perspective need to follow this approach since Latina religious activities should be conceptualized as part of U.S. third-world feminism enacting differential oppositional consciousness.

[16] bell hooks, *Feminist Theory: From Margin to Center* (Cambridge, Mass.: South End Press, 2000), 19.

[17] Chela Sandoval, "US Third-World Feminism: The Theory and Method of Oppositional Consciousness in the Postmodern World," in *Feminist Postcolonial Theory: A Reader*, ed. Reina Lewis and Sara Mills (New York: Routledge, 2003), 86.

[18] Sandoval, "US Third-World Feminism," 89.

[19] Sandoval, "US Third-World Feminism," 89 (emphasis in original).

[20] Emma Pérez, *The Decolonial Imaginary: Writing Chicanas into History* (Bloomington: Indiana University Press, 1999), 5.

FEMINIST HISTORY AS SUBALTERN HISTORY

Through the inclusion of U.S. third-world feminism, feminist history begins to work as a postcolonizing project. But it works not only in the challenge of hegemonic feminism but also challenges postcolonizing criticism. Recognizing this, Reina Lewis and Sara Mills maintain, "It is clear that current feminist postcolonial theory still exerts a pressure on mainstream postcolonial theory in its constant iteration of the necessity to consider gender issues."[21] This implies a movement of considering women as subaltern subjects and not as an extension of the male-subaltern. At the same time, the focus on differential consciousness makes it clear that historians need to look beyond the traditional representations of women of color within the narratives in order to dismantle those representations. As Chandra Talpade Mohanty explains, "The relationship between Women—a cultural and ideological composite Other constructed through diverse representational discourse (scientific, literary, juridical, linguistic, cinematic, etc.)—and women—real, material subjects of their collective histories—is one of the central questions the practice of feminist scholarship seeks to address."[22] Thus, feminist scholarship is closer to the practice within subaltern histories of evaluating the connections between the discursive representations of the subaltern and the real subaltern. The discursive representations of women of color within colonial discourses follow the museum historical education approach, which I referred to in the previous chapter. With the dismantling of colonial discourses, the historian is able to explore these connections, especially as they expose that "the discursively consensual homogeneity of 'women' as a group is mistaken for the historically specific material reality of groups of women."[23] Women, then, are not simple artifacts of history that can be fixed into a narrative as homogeneous, but through feminist history of the subaltern, the historian "must raise the question of woman as a structural rather than marginal issue in each of the many different types and cultures."[24]

[21] Reina Lewis and Sara Mills, "Introduction," in Lewis and Mills, *Feminist Postcolonial Theory*, 2.

[22] Chandra Talpade Mohanty, "Under Western Eyes: Feminist Scholarship and Colonial Discourses," in Lewis and Mills, *Feminist Postcolonial Theory*, 50.

[23] Mohanty, "Under Western Eyes," 53.

[24] Gayatri Chakravorty Spivak, "Subaltern Studies: Deconstructing Histor-

In order to be able to incorporate women as an intrinsic subject of the narratives, historians first have to search for that fragmented past present within traditional narratives. As with subaltern history, it is a matter of finding the spaces within the traditional narratives where the group "women" resides. "These interstitial gaps interrupt the linear model of time, and it is in such locations that oppositional, subaltern histories can be found."[25] Traditional histories silence the voices of the subaltern within these spaces. Emma Pérez argues that "these silences, when heard, become the negotiating spaces for the decolonizing subject."[26] When dis-covered, these spaces offer the historian the opportunity to see the breaks in traditional history. Latinas, as subaltern, live within these gaps, and through their everyday experiences they are able to enact differential oppositional consciousness from these spaces. The historian has the task of understanding these experiences as acts of subversion that prove the agency of Latinas, and thus avoid becoming simple historical artifacts. Hence, a different theoretical approach is needed to fit the Latina experience.

LATINA FEMINIST HISTORICAL ANALYSIS

In referring to the challenge that feminist history provides to the discipline of history, Joan Wallach Scott explains that, "Feminist history then becomes not just an attempt to correct or supplement an incomplete record of the past but a way of critically understanding how history operates as a site of the production of gender knowledge."[27] The possibility of this confronting mission is only presented because of the inclusion of theory within the historical work to the point that Scott argues that, "Although historians are not trained (in the United States at least) to be reflective or rigorous about their theory, I found it imperative to pursue theoretical questions in order to do feminist history."[28] As subaltern histories, Latina feminist historical approaches are also in need of new theories. These theories need to stand out against those used by hegemonic modes of

iography," in *Selected Subaltern Studies*, ed. Ranajit Guha and Gayatri Chakravorty Spivak (New York: Oxford University Press, 1988), 30.

[25] Pérez, *Decolonial Imaginary*, 5.

[26] Pérez, *Decolonial Imaginary*, 5.

[27] Scott, *Gender and the Politics*, 10.

[28] Scott, *Gender and the Politics*, 3.

knowledge. And, as mentioned before in chapter 5, Sonia Saldívar-Hull points to the importance of looking for theories outside the traditional places, like in *cuentos*, the voices of the marginalized and the non-recognized work of other Latina scholars.[29]

The basis for these new theories is founded in third-world feminism, which signals the existence of subjectivities within the interstices of the global movements toward liberation. In these instances of resistance against the systems of oppression, we can find theories that allow us to see Latinas as subaltern, struggling against their erasure by the male-dominated institutions within their physical environment and the traditional modes of knowledge within the discursive arena.

Now, in order to use third-world feminism, historians cannot keep doing history the same way because the discourses must change. In this regard, Saldívar-Hull reminds us that, "If feminist scholars, activists, and writers—who have lived under the *o* in *Chicano*—had to rely on the historical record written by men and male-identified women, Chicanas' roles in history would remain obscured."[30] In other words, it is important to look beyond the official documents. I am not implying that there is no value in these documents. On the contrary, new readings of these documents from the perspective of third-world feminism are essential, as they provide the historian a look into the silences within them. Now, a look at diaries, poems, letters, and other documents left by Latinas offer feminist historians a look into the world of Latinas beyond the monolithic constructions within official documents and reproduced by traditional history. Even further, Latina feminist historical analysis, as in lived religion, depends on the examination of the everyday experiences of Latinas. In her own examination of the methodologies within the development of Chicana feminist historical analysis, Saldívar-Hull acknowledges this evolution in the ways and places one can hear Latina voices:

> As I look back at these Chicano poems from the 1970s and my own early readings of them, I can see how once we had access to historical archives, reading Chicana identity politics could become more nuanced. The contemporary historians Vicki Ruiz, Antonia

[29] Saldívar-Hull, *Feminism on the Border*, 46.

[30] Saldívar-Hull, *Feminism on the Border*, 27 (emphasis in original).

> Castañeda, Deena González, Ramón Gutiérrez, George J. Sánchez, and Omar Valerio-Jiménez, to name just a few, work with traditional methodologies yet forge the emergent field of Chicana feminist history as they pose questions that earlier historians failed to ask. Turning to feminist theory and cultural studies, the new Chicana/o historians undertake gendered analyses of historical records. Other cultural workers—poets, fiction writers, literary critics—seek innovative methods to uncover and recover history. The three Chicanas whose texts I examine closely in the following chapters—Gloria Anzaldúa, Sandra Cisneros, and Helena María Viramontes—investigate domestic and other female spaces as they seek additional sources of history. These women, who produced their literary texts in the 1980s, discovered alternative archives in the gossip and rumors for which Chicanas are criticized and through which they are silenced; in the lacunae of family stories that tell of confined grandmothers and abused great-grandmothers; and the late-night kitchen-table talks with Mexican immigrants to the barrios of the United States.[31]

Following this evolution in methodologies, I argue that in order to find these voices within the religious experiences of Latinas/os, historians need to draw on ritual studies, lived religion, material culture, and other cultural studies approaches. Through the use of methodologies from a third-world feminism perspective, historians of Latina/o religions will uncover Latinas as a subaltern subject engaged in everyday religious experiences, inside or outside the religious institutions, that challenge their previous representations and offer a historical window into the whole Latina/o religious experience.

LATINA FEMINIST HISTORICAL RELIGIOUS DISCOURSE

The inclusion of a feminist perspective within much of the literature in the field of Latina/o religious history mainly has followed the approach of adding several women's names and stories to the narratives. They have not included gender as a category of analysis or employed third-world feminism as a theoretical tool. For example, the importance of women in Protestant missionary activities—especially in the areas of education, medicine, and social engagement—and in the development of rituals and social activism

[31] Saldívar-Hull, *Feminism on the Border*, 25.

in the Catholic Church, has been widely documented, and many of the projects within this discipline include some information regarding these aspects. But, with few exceptions, these works have not been constructed on the basis of feminist criticism. The absence of this perspective locates women as historical artifacts and not as active participants in the construction of the history of the community. Through third-world feminism, women acquire subjectivity and their religious activities are evaluated as subversive activities, grounded in differential oppositional consciousness.

The reasons for the absence of gender analysis, especially in the early literature on Latina/o religious histories, are several, including the lack of material available in order to construct a particular examination. But as valid as this reason might seem to be, it can be argued that the whole field of Latina/o religious history is marked by limited available sources, and this has not stopped scholars from producing historical works. The actual *absence* of documentation implies an exercise of power in order to erase, hide, or silence the past. It is in these gaps that historians find the subaltern, and thus need to change their approaches in order to listen to the voices within these spaces. Gender becomes one of those possible approaches that would expose the gaps and focus on the subaltern within them. Sarah Deutsch's *No Separate Refuge* provides a possible model of how to include gender as part of the methodological approach.[32] In the first pages of the book, she acknowledges the complexity and rareness of her task. Deutsch asserts that "written history of female minorities or 'ethnics' is rare, that of Chicanas or Hispanic women rarer though increasing, and of Chicanas or Hispanic women in Colorado virtually non-existent."[33] Still, she ventures into the project using gender as a category of analysis in the exploration of the contact and exchange between Latinas/os and Anglo-Americans in Colorado.

Conventional wisdom about Latinas identifies their subordination at home, but after going beyond the mere reading of the available literature and interpreting the silences within them, Deutsch found a different version of women's experiences. She reread

[32] See Sarah Deutsch, *No Separate Refuge: Culture, Class, and Gender on an Anglo-Hispanic Frontier in the American Southwest, 1880–1940* (New York: Oxford University Press, 1987).

[33] Deutsch, *No Separate Refuge*, 11.

existing materials through the women's lenses and found that earlier interpretations of the data hid not only the presence of women but their agency. Deutsch confronted these interpretations and discovered the silences within them. She revised and re-envisioned the narrative, and suggests, "The resulting revision, however, changed not only the picture of Hispanic women's experience, but the entire picture of the Hispanic-Anglo contact, the strategies and the possibilities for each party."[34] So the inclusion of gender not only unmasks conventional wisdom and stereotypes about women, but also reconstructs the larger Latina/o religious history.

In her work, Deutsch uses gender as a category of analysis "not isolated from the rest of the study but causally linked to it."[35] And it is through this integration that she not only uncovers a new picture of the Latina religious experience but also finds that historians have not looked beyond traditional male-oriented models in order to reach this dis-covery. She states:

> Middle-class Anglo women and men, social workers, educators, churchgoers, and farmers' wives, focused their missionary and Americanizing efforts—and their hostility—on working class Chicanas as they did on women of other minorities. And Chicana work patterns became, as did those of women from other ethnic groups, an intimate part of the group's survival strategy. The reliance of the debate regarding change and continuity on old male-oriented models of intercultural relations has distracted historians from changes occurring within female activities, even when the forms seem most stable. Furthermore, those older models have hidden the impact of changes in women's activities on the group as a whole, an impact crucial to the interaction of the group with Anglo society.[36]

In other words, the incorporation of the issue of gender forces a re-visioning of previous statements and presupposed information, and it deconstructs the existing models of interpretation. Latinas are, then, seen as subjects, agents of their own history. I argue that the first step is to revisit the historical archives (official documents) and

[34] Deutsch, *No Separate Refuge,* 11.
[35] Deutsch, *No Separate Refuge,* 11.
[36] Deutsch, *No Separate Refuge,* 11.

reread them in order to find the gaps as pertains to Latina involvement in the development of religious experiences and the evolution of the communities themselves. In the larger scheme, it is important to remember that this revisiting cannot entail a simple look through the lens of gender, but must engage all the lenses of third-world feminism, which include gender, race, class, and global resistance against systems of power.

After this first step, the dis-covery of the hidden spaces within the archives and the traditional narratives, historians are forced to look beyond them. For example, Lara Medina, in her groundbreaking work on Las Hermanas, provides the history of a subaltern challenge to the institution and the leaders of their own community by integrating "oral history and archival research."[37] Through an "in-depth study of Chicanas and Latinas as religious leaders and agents of transformation, it offers an interdisciplinary examination of religion, ethnicity, gender, and politics."[38] This is an example of a project in which the feminist analysis of history provides a challenge not only to the traditional history of the Catholic Church in the United States, but also to the way Latina/o religious history has been developing within the last few decades. Medina highlights the agency of Latinas within their religious activities, and how their leadership is able to challenge the institution and enact change. These activities, once seen through the lenses of third-world feminism, illustrate acts of differential oppositional consciousness, which cannot be hidden anymore within Latina/o religious histories.

On the other hand, most of the religious experiences of women cannot be found in organized forms of resistance, as in the organization of Las Hermanas. In the case of Latina/o religious history, historians need to look into the everyday religious experiences of Latinas through which they forge spaces of subjectivity. One cannot focus simply on the leadership of women, or lack thereof, within institutional structures. These positions are important, and they represent certain developments in the role of women, but it is within the unofficial leadership positions in religious communities that Latinas exercise their agency. These become spaces of resistance, in which Latinas are able to re-envision their location within the community,

[37] Lara Medina, *Las Hermanas: Chicana/Latina Religious-Political Activism in the U.S. Catholic Church* (Philadelphia: Temple University Press, 2004), 7.

[38] Medina, *Las Hermanas,* 6.

and from which historians are able to revise the historical narratives. It is not a matter of supplementing the traditional narratives in order to fill the gaps with these voices, because the fact is that these voices irrupt into the scene, breaking apart the normative metanarrative. Since the actors change and the hegemonic ideology behind the actions is revealed, I am not talking about a mere remodeling but a reconstruction.

Third-world feminism, with its focus on race and class, also forces historians to look in different places for these religious experiences, as they are not just located within particular rituals or in specific positions inside or outside the religious institution. As mentioned above, a diversity of places exist wherein one finds these voices. The same is true for Latina religious experiences. Lara Medina explains:

> Whether they are santería priestesses communing with orishas, curanderas healing the sick, Catholic sisters and laywomen challenging racism and sexism, Latinas doing theology, educators passing on the faith, temple keepers cleaning and beautifying sanctuaries, Protestant ministers preaching and organizing, keepers of the sweat lodge tradition, sun dancers, or ritual planners, Latinas reflect the great diversity of religious experience.[39]

Again, the dis-covery of all these spaces of subversion do not simply open the discourse to the *presence* of Latinas within the religious experience, but they actually expand the larger field of Latina/o religious history. Because most of these activities are outside the range of institutional power, or even outside the focus on Christian experiences that most Latina/o religious histories have followed, they would be left unexamined, hidden, and forgotten, as if they were not representative of Latina/o religious experiences. Hence, the use of third-world feminism within historical analysis provides a break from the previous limits of historical examination, dis-covering places of resistance that at the same time serve to unlock memories about the diverse religious experiences that form Latina/o religious identities.

Here, I am not arguing that all *marginalized* religious activities by Latinas provide an insight into the ways one can totally transform the larger field of Latina/o religious history. My argument, in a more modest way, resembles Chandra Talpade Mohanty's focus on

[39] Medina, "Women," 299.

the particular social/material experiences of women. She explains: "My claim is not that all marginalized locations yield crucial knowledge about power and inequity, but that within a tightly integrated capitalist system, the particular standpoint of poor indigenous and Third World/South women provides the most inclusive viewing of systemic power."[40] In the same way, and because Latinas are involved in the majority of Latina/o religious experiences, by focusing on them as historical agents, one is able to view the larger picture. In everyday life experiences, the subaltern is capable of challenging the structures of power, and thus subaltern historians have the responsibility of focusing on these and other unofficial *texts* (e.g., songs, *testimonios*, rumors, poems, diaries) that provide a window into this experience of subversion. Leaving them out would not simply imply that those discourses are different than the ones that include these feminist perspectives, but that the former may serve as reproductions of colonial discourses that hide oppositional difference.

BEYOND THE DISCURSIVE

In her essay "The Project of Feminist Epistemology: Perspectives from a Nonwestern Feminist," Uma Narayan maintains that, "The inclusion of women's perspective will not merely amount to women participating in greater numbers in the existing practice of science and knowledge, but it will change the very nature of these activities and their self-understanding."[41] The integration of third-world feminism within Latina/o religious history would definitively lead to this challenge of established common perceptions, especially as it confronts modernity. For example, as Norma Alarcón states, "By having women be the subject of knowledge, the so-called objectivity of men is brought into question."[42] As part of its challenge to modern notions of *reality*, third-world feminism would challenge the traditional way historical discourses are constructed. As in the case of

[40] Chandra Talpade Mohanty, *Feminism Without Borders: Decolonizing Theory, Practicing Solidarity* (Durham, N.C.: Duke University Press, 2003), 232.

[41] Uma Narayan, "The Project of Feminist Epistemology: Perspectives from a Nonwestern Feminist," in *Feminist Theory Reader: Local and Global Perspectives*, ed. Carole R. McCann and Seung-Kyung Kim (New York: Routledge, 2003), 308.

[42] Norma Alarcón, "The Theoretical Subject(s) of *This Bridge Called My Back* and Anglo-American Feminism," in McCann and Kim, *Feminist Theory Reader*, 408.

lived religion, third-world feminism encourages historical discourses based not on the modernist project of truth, but on oppositional difference.

But third-world feminism not only challenges knowledge and the way historical narratives are constructed. It actually challenges the significance of historical practice by locating the historian's work within the feminist project, as a mode of praxis. It this sense, the historian's work becomes more than an academic task; it becomes a political engagement. Chandra Talpade Mohanty argues that "feminist scholarly practices exist within relations of power—relations which they counter, redefine or even implicitly support. There can, of course, be no apolitical scholarship."[43] Historians within this project should be committed to feminism as "a struggle to end sexist oppression," and as "a struggle to eradicate the ideology of domination that permeates Western culture on various levels, as well as a commitment to reorganizing society so that the self-development of people can take precedence over imperialism, economic expansion, and material desires."[44] I argue that this approach relocates the historian's work to the sociopolitical arena. In the same way that particular social movements create change within society and become sites where knowledge is constructed, historical narratives produce and reproduce knowledge that affects the movements in society. Following third-world feminism, historians recognize their status as producers of knowledge, but the produced knowledge is not objective or universal. On the contrary, historians become social workers, producing knowledge that transforms society toward an egalitarian reality.

Historians would construct self-critical discourses, as described in the previous chapter, that not only reveal the voices of women and men that have been silenced, but also provide an exposition of the attitudes and ideologies that have prevented these voices from acquiring subjectivity within the discursive arena. These narratives would offer the subaltern a window to their past and an understanding of those principles that sustain domination. In the case of Latina/o religious history, one is able to see, among other things, Latinas' subjectivity in the religious experiences of the community while also locating the ideology and attitudes of both the

[43] Mohanty, "Under Western Eyes," 50.

[44] hooks, *Feminist Theory*, 26.

institutions of power and the male-dominated Latina/o culture that have silenced their voices. For example, Medina's work on Las Hermanas not only "expands our understanding of the role that women and religion have played and continue to play in the struggle for self-determination," but also uncovers and exposes the male-centered attitudes that still continue marginalizing Latina leadership.[45] In the same way, a look at *curanderas* and *santeras* provides details of spaces where Latinas exercise their agency while, as mentioned above, also expanding the field of Latina/o religious history beyond its traditional focus on Christianity, exposing that prejudicial ideology that has silenced others within Latina/o religious communities. With this double-edged approach, historians side with the struggle of the subaltern against the hegemonic systems of power that promote domination, even if these are embedded within sectors of the subaltern experience (e.g., *machismo*, religious discrimination, racism).

[45] Medina, *Las Hermanas*, 11.

CONCLUSION
THEORIZING AND *CONOCIMIENTO*

Michel-Rolph Trouillot asserts that "theories of history rarely examine in detail the concrete production of specific narratives."[1] Because this assessment fits perfectly with the development of U.S. religious historiography, the dominant discourses within this field have not only been able to consolidate their power but also to reproduce it, as there have not been many works examining the construction of the narratives. Traditional U.S. religious historiography has been confronted and revised, but its colonialist character is still present, mainly because the Protestant-Puritan experience has remained as the starting point of the traditional narrative. This colonialist character provokes the supremacy of a black/white paradigm and the lack of attention to issues of race, class, and gender beyond this paradigm. Even when revisions open the field to new topics, themes, and new perspectives in U.S. religious history, the Anglo-American cultural framework still dominates the field. As a result, I argue that in order to engage in a historical project that seeks postcolonization of the discourse and the discipline, historians and philosophers of history need to pay attention to the construction of narratives and the ideologies behind them.

The analysis of old and new approaches, themes, and topics within U.S. religious historiography provides an overview of theories and methods employed. The deconstruction of these theories and methods will then lead to the development of fresh perspectives,

[1] Michel-Rolph Trouillot, *Silencing the Past: Power and the Production of History* (Boston: Beacon, 1995), 22.

new considerations, methodologies, epistemologies, and even a more critical edge, all of which are needed within the field. Thus, I offer a new discursive approach to the writing of U.S. Latina/o religious history. Constructed as a counter-discourse from a subaltern perspective, U.S. Latina/o religious history will be able to challenge the colonialist aspect at the center of U.S. religious historiography. I suggest that a postcolonizing perspective to the study and writing of U.S. Latina/o religious history would develop a theoretical scaffold that would decolonize the field of U.S. religious history and locate U.S. Latina/o religious history as such a counter-discourse. Thus, in the last section of this book, I introduce two possible approaches to develop historical projects within a postcolonizing perspective. The key in both lived religion and feminist approaches is the conception of the work from a subaltern perspective without essentializing that subaltern. This means that every project needs to see itself as one of many and not as the ultimate truth on the topic. In order to be able to build this kind of project, we then need to understand theory in a different light, not from a Western colonialist perspective, and dismantle the traditional knowledges that have dominated the field.

Gloria Anzaldúa points out in the preface to *Making Face, Making Soul/Haciendo Caras: Creative and Critical Perspectives by Feminists of Color* that there is a need for theories from outside the dominant academic circles. She finds that while theory "is a set of knowledges" and "some of these knowledges have been kept from us," people of color, and women of color in particular, need to transform the theorizing space with new methodologies and approaches and "not allow whitemen and women solely to occupy it."[2] Anzaldúa goes on further to assert:

> *Necesitamos teorías* that will rewrite history using race, class, gender and ethnicity as categories of analysis, theories that cross borders, that blur boundaries—new kinds of theories with new theorizing methods. We need theories that will point out ways to maneuver between our particular experiences and the necessity of forming our own categories and theoretical models for the

[2] Gloria Anzaldúa, "Haciendo Caras, Una Entrada," in *Making Face, Making Soul/Haciendo Caras: Creative and Critical Perspectives by Feminists of Color*, ed. Gloria Anzaldúa (San Francisco: Aunt Lute Books, 1990), xxv.

> patterns we uncover. We need theories that examine the implications of situations and look at what's behind them.[3]

Through these new theories we confront Western epistemology and dis-cover new categories and modes of interpretation. We have to reconstruct knowledges, subaltern knowledges, in order to deconstruct traditional colonial discourses. Thus, it is important to step away from "traditional" conceptions of knowledge and reconstruct them in terms of *conocimiento,* which is "skeptical of reason and rationality . . . [and which] questions conventional knowledge's current categories, classifications, and contents."[4]

Conocimiento comes when we understand our experiences, our stories, as processes for a new path that leads toward the postcolonization of discourses, when truth is accepted as a process and not the result of the discourses. We need to be open to this process because, as Anzaldúa argues, it "guides your (our) feet along the path, gives you (us) el ánimo to dedicate yourself (ourselves) to transforming perceptions of reality, and thus the conditions of life."[5] The process of/toward *conocimiento* involves the transformation of the traditional colonial paradigms and colonial discourses by deconstructing them and building an egalitarian system: a move toward liberation. In this sense, it is not simply to talk about a change in the characters and the themes, but a complete transformation in the understanding of history as a colonial enterprise. This transformation does not happen by trying to explain the colonial relationship or by using Western conceptions of knowledge to theorize about it. Through *conocimiento,* however, we can see beyond historical narratives of oppression and build new counter-narratives, postcolonizing stories that help decolonize both the colonized and the colonizer.

In the past decades, through postmodern, postcolonial, feminist, queer, and other types of analysis, major colonial and imperialist discourses have been examined and challenged. Traditional histories have been deconstructed and the knowledge they have put forward

[3] Anzaldúa, "Haciendo Caras," xxv–xxvi.

[4] Gloria Anzaldúa, "Now Let Us Shift . . . The Path of Conocimiento . . . Inner Work, Public Acts," in *This Bridge We Call Home: Radical Visions for Transformation,* ed. Gloria E. Anzaldúa and AnaLouise Keating (New York: Routledge, 2002), 541.

[5] Anzaldúa, "Now Let Us Shift," 540.

has been challenged. But while Anzaldúa expresses hope that "the binaries of colored/white, female/male, mind/body are collapsing,"[6] I do not see these or any other colonial discourses as destroyed, only reconfigured to fit contemporary neo-colonial relationships. Thus, binaries may be challenged, histories deconstructed, and stories uncovered, but the colonial discourses that support the colonial interpretations are only reinterpreted and still carry the whole universalist/normative character. Transformation and/or destruction of these discourses has only occurred in the minds of those in power, who have been forced to change their traditional oppressive/colonial modes of representation of the Other for new modes of representation. In spite of new discourses that open the door for silenced voices to come to the forefront, colonial modes of representation and traditional historicizing are still determining which historical narratives are responsible for the creation of normative knowledges. An engagement in the process of *conocimiento* would break these constructs.

Achieving *conocimiento* involves the analysis of our stories and experiences. But, in order to go back and reread the stories and recover a memory, the lenses we use to reread our past/present have to be transformed—our mental perceptions have to be decolonized. Anzaldúa writes:

> Breaking out of your mental and emotional prison and deepening the range of perception enables you to link inner reflection and vision—the mental, emotional, instinctive, imaginal, spiritual, and subtle bodily awareness—with social, political action and lived experiences to generate subversive knowledges. These *conocimientos* challenge official and conventional ways of looking at the world, ways set up by those benefiting from such constructions.[7]

Deconstructing that system requires that we break away from our mental constructs in order to reread our experiences and stories from a transformative and postcolonizing perspective. In this sense, it is not a matter of just telling our stories, but telling our stories from the perspective of the colonized and not the colonizer. Using theory to deconstruct the colonial discourses, following an ethical perspective

[6] Anzaldúa, "Now Let Us Shift," 541.

[7] Anzaldúa, "Now Let Us Shift," 542.

to construct new discourses, and allowing the stories from silenced communities to be told are the steps toward *conocimiento*. While traditional historical discourses, which lack self-reflection, have the objective of representing a universal and absolute truth, through *conocimiento* we can reconfigure their conclusions as particular perspectives, not normative knowledges. One of the ways actually to challenge those normative knowledges is to confront the actual narratives through new subaltern discourses, new ways of reading and writing.

I hope that the examples of new theorizing I offer in this book open the door to *nuevos conocimientos* and the development of Latina/o religious historical discourses from a subaltern perspective.

SELECTED BIBLIOGRAPHY

Adam, Ian, and Helen Tiffin, eds. *Past the Last Post: Theorizing Post-colonialism and Post-modernism*. Calgary: University of Calgary Press, 1990.

Ahlstrom, Sydney E. *A Religious History of the American People*. New Haven, Conn.: Yale University Press, 1972.

Albanese, Catherine L. *America: Religions and Religion*. Belmont, Calif.: Wadsworth, 1992.

Aldama, Arturo J., and Naomi H. Quiñonez, eds. *Decolonial Voices: Chicana and Chicano Cultural Studies in the 21st Century*. Bloomington: Indiana University Press, 2002.

Ammerman, Nancy T., ed. *Everyday Religion: Observing Modern Religious Lives*. New York: Oxford University Press, 2006.

Anzaldúa, Gloria. *Borderlands/La Frontera: The New Mestiza*. San Francisco: Aunt Lute Books, 1987.

———, ed. *Making Face, Making Soul/Haciendo Caras: Creative and Critical Perspectives by Feminists of Color*. San Francisco: Aunt Lute Books, 1990.

Anzaldúa, Gloria E., and AnaLouise Keating. *This Bridge We Call Home: Radical Visions for Transformation*. New York: Routledge, 2002.

Anzaldúa, Gloria, and Cherríe Moraga, eds. *This Bridge Called My Back: Writings by Radical Women of Color*. New York: Kitchen Table Press, 1983.

Appleby, Joyce, Lynn Hunt, and Margaret Jacobs. *Telling the Truth about History*. New York: Norton, 1994.

Aquino, María Pilar, Daisy L. Machado, and Jeanette Rodríguez, eds. *A Reader in Latina Feminist Theology: Religion and Justice*. Austin: University of Texas Press, 2002.

Ashcroft, Bill, Gareth Griffiths, and Helen Tiffin. *The Empire Writes Back: Theory and Practice in Post-colonial Literatures*. London: Routledge, 1989.

———. *Post-colonial Studies: The Key Concepts*. London: Routledge, 2000.

———, eds. *The Post-colonial Studies Reader*. London: Routledge, 1995.

Avalos, Hector, ed. *Introduction to the U.S. Latina and Latino Religious Experience*. Boston: Brill Academic, 2004.

Bacon, Leonard W. *A History of American Christianity*. New York: Christian Literature, 1897.

Badger, R. Reid, and Lawrence A. Clayton, eds. *Alabama and the Borderlands: From Prehistory to Statehood*. Tuscaloosa: University of Alabama Press, 1985.

Badillo, David A. *Latinos and the New Immigrant Church*. Baltimore: Johns Hopkins University Press, 2006.

Bahti, Timothy. *Allegories of History: Literary Historiography after Hegel*. Baltimore: Johns Hopkins University Press, 1992.

Baird, Robert. *Religion in America; or An Account of the Origin, Relation to the State, and Present Conditions of the Evangelical Churches in the United States with Notices of the Unevangelical Denominations*. New York: Harper & Brothers, 1856.

Barker, Francis, Peter Hulme, and Margaret Iversen, eds. *Colonial Discourse/Postcolonial Theory*. Manchester, UK: Manchester University Press, 1994.

Barton, Paul. *Hispanic Methodists, Presbyterians, and Baptists in Texas*. Austin: University of Texas Press, 2006.

Barton, Paul, and David Maldonado Jr., eds. *Hispanic Christianity within Mainline Protestant Traditions: A Bibliography*. Decatur, Ga.: Asociación para la Educación Teológica Hispana, 1998.

Benjamin, Walter. *Illuminations*. Edited by Hannah Arendt. Translated by Harry Zohn. New York: Schocken, 1985.

Bently, Michael, ed. *Companion to Historiography*. London: Routledge, 1997.

Beverley, John, Michael Aronna, and José Oviedo, eds. *The Postmodernism Debate in Latin America*. Durham, N.C.: Duke University Press, 1995.

Bhabha, Homi. *The Location of Culture*. London: Routledge, 1994.

Billington, Ray Allen. *The Far Western Frontier: 1830–1860*. New York: Harper & Row, 1956.

———. *Land of Savagery, Land of Promise: The European Image of the American Frontier in the Nineteenth Century*. Norman: University of Oklahoma Press, 1981.

Bolton, Herbert Eugene. *The Spanish Borderlands: A Chronicle of Old Florida and the Southwest*. Albuquerque: University of New Mexico Press, 1996. Originally published by Yale University Press, 1921.

Bonilla, Frank, Edwin Meléndez, Rebecca Morales, and María de los Angeles Torres, eds. *Borderless Borders: U.S. Latinos, Latin Americans, and the Paradox of Interdependence*. Philadelphia: Temple University Press, 1998.

Bowden, Henry Warner, and P. C. Kemeny, eds. *American Church History: A Reader*. Nashville: Abingdon, 1998.

Boyer, Paul. "Testimony Time: Historians Reflect on Current Issues in American Religious History." *Evangelical Studies Bulletin* 15, no. 3 (1998): 1–5.

Brackenridge, R. Douglas, and Francisco García-Treto. *Iglesia Presbiteriana: A History of Presbyterians and Mexican Americans in the Southwest*. San Antonio, Tex.: Trinity University Press, 1987.

Brauer, Jerald C. *Protestantism in America: A Narrative History*. Philadelphia: Westminster, 1953.

———, ed. *Reinterpretation in American Church History.* Chicago: University of Chicago Press, 1968.

———. "Review of *A Religious History of the American People,* by Sydney E. Ahlstrom." *Church History* 42, no. 3 (1973): 406–9.

Breisach, Ernst. *Historiography: Ancient, Medieval & Modern.* Chicago: University of Chicago Press, 1994.

Brueggemann, Walter. *The Prophetic Imagination.* 2nd ed. Minneapolis: Fortress, 2001.

Burke, Peter. *The French Historical Revolution: The Annales School 1929–89.* Cambridge: Polity, 1990.

———, ed. *New Perspectives in Historical Writing.* University Park: Pennsylvania State University Press, 1991.

Busto, Rudy V. *King Tiger: The Religious Vision of Reies López Tijerina.* Albuquerque: University of New Mexico Press, 2005.

Butler, Jon. *Awash in a Sea of Faith: Christianizing the American People.* Cambridge, Mass.: Harvard University Press, 1990.

Butler, Jon, and Harry S. Stout, eds. *Religion in American History: A Reader.* New York: Oxford University Press, 1998.

Calderón, Héctor, and José David Saldívar, eds. *Criticism in the Borderlands: Studies in Chicano Literature, Culture, and Ideology.* Durham, N.C.: Duke University Press, 1991.

Castañeda, Antonia I. "Gender, Race, and Culture: Spanish-Mexican Women in the Historiography of Frontier California." *Frontiers* 11, no. 1 (1990): 8–20.

Castro-Gómez, Santiago, and Eduardo Mendieta. *Teorías Sin Disciplina. Latinoamericanismo, Poscolonialidad y Globalización en Debate.* Mexico City: Miguel Angel Porrua, 1998.

Castro-Gómez, Santiago, Oscar Guardiola-Rivera, and Carmen Millán de Benavides. *Pensar (en) los Intersticios: Teoría y Práctica de la Crítica Poscolonial.* Santa Fe de Bogotá, Columbia: Instituto Pensar, 1999.

Chakrabarty, Dipesh. *Provincializing Europe: Postcolonial Thought and Historical Difference.* Princeton, N.J.: Princeton University Press, 2000.

Chartier, Roger. *On the Edge of the Cliff: History, Language and Practices.* Translated by Lydia G. Cochrane. Baltimore: Johns Hopkins University Press, 1997.

Cruz, Samuel. *Masked Africanisms: Puerto Rican Pentecostalism.* Dubuque, Iowa: Kendall Hunt, 2005.

Daniels, David. "Teaching the History of U.S. Christianity in a Global Perspective." *Theological Education* 29, no. 2 (1993): 91–111.

Darder, Antonia, and Rodolfo D. Torres, eds. *The Latino Studies Reader: Culture, Economy, and Society.* Malden, Mass.: Blackwell, 1998.

Davis, Kenneth G., Eduardo C. Fernández, and Verónica Méndez, eds. *United States Hispanic Catholics: Trends and Works, 1990–2000.* Scranton, Pa.: University of Scranton Press, 2002.

de Certeau, Michel. *The Writing of History.* Translated by Tom Conley. New York: Columbia University Press, 1988.

De La Torre, Miguel A., and Gastón Espinosa, eds. *Rethinking Latino(a) Religion and Identity.* Cleveland, Ohio: Pilgrim Press, 2006.

De León, Arnoldo. *They Called Them Greasers: Anglo Attitudes toward Mexicans in Texas, 1821–1900.* Austin: University of Texas Press, 1983.

Del Castillo, Adelaida R., ed. *Between Borders: Essays on Mexicana/Chicana History.* Encino, Calif.: Floricanto Press, 1990.

Delgado, Richard, and Jean Stefancic, eds. *The Latino/a Condition: A Critical Reader.* New York: New York University Press, 1998.

Deutsch, Sarah. *No Separate Refuge: Culture, Class, and Gender on an Anglo-Hispanic Frontier in the American Southwest, 1880–1940.* New York: Oxford University Press, 1987.

Díaz-Quiñones, Arcadio. *La Memoria Rota: Ensayos Sobre Cultura y Política.* Río Piedras, Puerto Rico: Ediciones Huracán, 1993.

Dilthey, Wilhelm. *Gesammelte Schriften.* Leipzig: B.G. Teubner, 1914.

———. *Introduction to the Human Sciences: An Attempt to Lay a Foundation for the Study of Society and History.* Translated by Ramon J. Betanzos. Detroit: Wayne State University Press, 1988.

Dirlik, Arif. *The Postcolonial Aura: Third World Criticism in the Age of Global Capitalism.* Boulder, Colo.: Westview, 1997.

———. *Postmodernity's Histories: The Past as Legacy and Project.* Lanham, Md.: Rowman & Littlefield, 2000.

Dolan, Jay P. *The American Catholic Experience: A History from Colonial Times to the Present.* Garden City, N.Y.: Image, 1985.

Dolan, Jay P., and Allan Figueroa Deck, eds. *Hispanic Catholic Culture in the U.S.: Issues and Concerns.* Notre Dame: University of Notre Dame Press, 1994.

Dolan, Jay P., and Gilberto M. Hinojosa, eds. *Mexican Americans and the Catholic Church, 1900–1965.* Notre Dame: University of Notre Dame Press, 1994.

Dolan, Jay P., and Jaime R. Vidal, eds. *Puerto Rican and Cuban Catholics in the U.S., 1900–1965.* Notre Dame: University of Notre Dame Press, 1994.

Dorchester, Daniel. *Christianity in the United States from the First Settlement Down to the Present Time.* New York: Phillips & Hunt, 1888.

Droysen, Johann Gustav. *Historik.* Stuttgart: Frommann-Holzboog, 1977.

———. *Outline of the Principles of History.* Translated by E. Benjamin Andrews. Boston: Ginn, 1893.

Du Bois, W. E. B. *The Souls of Black Folk.* Chicago: A. C. McClurg, 1903.

Dussel, Enrique. *Ética Comunitaria.* Madrid: Ediciones Paulinas, 1986.

———. *The Invention of the Americas: Eclipse of "the Other" and the Myth of Modernity.* Translated by Michael D. Barber. New York: Continuum, 1995.

Espín, Orlando O. *The Faith of the People: Theological Reflections on Popular Catholicism.* Maryknoll, N.Y.: Orbis, 1997.

Fanon, Frantz. *The Wretched of the Earth.* New York: Grover, 1963.

Foucault, Michel. *The Archaeology of Knowledge & the Discourse on Language.* Translated by A. M. Sheridan Smith. New York: Pantheon, 1972.

———. *Power/Knowledge: Selected Interviews and Other Writings, 1972–1977.* Edited by Colin Gordon. Translated by Colin Gordon, Leo Marshall, John Mepham, and Kate Soper. New York: Pantheon, 1980.

Fukuyama, Francis. *The End of History and the Last Man.* New York: Avon, 1992.

García, Mario T. *Católicos: Resistance and Affirmation in Chicano Catholic History.* Austin: University of Texas Press, 2008.

García Verduzco, Pablo. *Bosquejo Histórico del Metodismo Mexicano en Texas y la Frontera de México.* Nashville: Cokesbury, 1933.

Gates, Henry Louis Jr., ed. *"Race," Writing, and Difference.* Chicago: University of Chicago Press, 1986.

Gaustad, Edwin S. *Religion in America: History and Historiography.* Washington, D.C.: American Historical Association, 1973.

———. *A Religious History of America.* New rev. ed. San Francisco: Harper San Francisco, 1990.

Gilderhus, Mark T. *History and Historians: A Historiographical Introduction.* Upper Saddle River, N.J.: Prentice Hall, 2000.

González, Justo, ed. *En Nuestra Propia Lengua: Una Historia del Metodismo Unido Hispano.* Nashville: Abingdon, 1991.

Gracia, Jorge J. E. *Hispanic/Latino Identity: A Philosophical Perspective.* Malden, Mass.: Blackwell, 2000.

Gracia, Jorge J. E., and Pablo De Greiff, eds. *Hispanics/Latinos in the United States: Ethnicity, Race, and Rights.* New York: Routledge, 2000.

Green, Anna, and Kathleen Troup. *The Houses of History: A Critical Reader in Twentieth-Century History and Theory.* New York: New York University Press, 1999.

Griswold Del Castillo, Richard. *The Treaty of Guadalupe Hidalgo: A Legacy of Conflict.* Norman: University of Oklahoma Press, 1990.

Grivalja, Joshua. *A History of Mexican Baptists in Texas, 1881–1981.* Dallas: Baptist General Convention of Texas, 1982.

Guha, Ranajit, and Gayatri Chakravorty Spivak, eds. *Selected Subaltern Studies.* New York: Oxford University Press, 1988.

Hackett, David G., ed. *Religion and American Culture: A Reader.* New York: Routledge, 1995.

Hall, David D., ed. *Lived Religion in America: Toward a History of Practice.* Princeton, N.J.: Princeton University Press, 1997.

Hall, Stuart, and Bram Gieben. *Formations of Modernity.* Cambridge, UK: Polity, 1992.

Handy, Robert T. *A History of the Churches in the United States and Canada.* New York: Oxford University Press, 1977.

Hardt, Michael, and Antonio Negri. *Empire.* Cambridge, Mass.: Harvard University Press, 2000.

Haselden, Kyle. *Death of a Myth: New Locus for Spanish American Faith.* New York: Friendship Press, 1964.

Herberg, Will. *Protestant-Catholic-Jew: An Essay in American Religious Sociology.* Garden City, N.Y.: Anchor, 1955.

Hicks, D. Emily. *Border Writing: The Multidimensional Text.* Minneapolis: University of Minnesota Press, 1991.

Hietala, Thomas R. *Manifest Design: Anxious Aggrandizement in Late Jacksonian America.* Ithaca, N.Y.: Cornell University Press, 1985.

Holland, Clifton L. *The Religious Dimension in Hispanic Los Angeles: A Protestant Case Study.* South Pasadena, Calif.: William Carey Library, 1974.

hooks, bell. *Feminist Theory: From Margin to Center.* Cambridge, Mass.: South End Press, 2000.

Hudson, Winthrop S. *American Protestantism.* Chicago: University of Chicago Press, 1961.

———. *Religion in America.* New York: Charles Scribner's Sons, 1965.

Hudson, Winthrop S., and John Corrigan. *Religion in America: An Historical Account of the Development of American Religious Life.* Upper Saddle River, N.J.: Prentice Hall, 1999.

Iggers, Georg G. *Historiography in the Twentieth Century: From Scientific Objectivity to the Postmodern Challenge.* Hanover, N.H.: Wesleyan University Press, 1997.

Iggers Georg G., and James M. Powell, eds. *Leopold von Ranke and the Shaping of the Historical Discipline.* Syracuse, N.Y.: Syracuse University Press, 1990.

Irvin, Dale. *Christian Histories, Christian Traditioning: Rendering Accounts.* Maryknoll, N.Y.: Orbis, 1998.

Irvin, Dale T., and Akintunde E. Akinade, eds. *The Agitated Mind of God: The Theology of Kosuke Koyama.* Maryknoll, N.Y.: Orbis, 1996.

Isaac, Rhys. *The Transformation of Virginia, 1740–1790.* Chapel Hill: University of North Carolina Press, 1982.

Isasi-Díaz, Ada María, and Fernando F. Segovia, eds. *Hispanic/Latino Theology: Challenge and Promise.* Minneapolis: Fortress, 1996.

Jacobsen, Douglas, and William Vance Trollinger Jr., eds. *Re-forming the Center: American Protestantism, 1900 to the Present.* Grand Rapids: Eerdmans, 1998.

Jameson, Fredric. *Postmodernism; or, The Cultural Logic of Late Capitalism.* Durham, N.C.: Duke University Press, 1991.

Jameson, Fredric, and Masao Miyoshi, eds. *The Cultures of Globalization.* Durham, N.C.: Duke University Press, 1998.

Jenkins, Keith. *On "What Is History?" From Carr and Elton to Rorty and White.* London: Routledge, 1995.

———, ed. *The Postmodern History Reader.* London: Routledge, 1997.

Joyce, Patrick. "History and Post-modernism, I." *Past and Present: A Journal of Historical Studies* 133 (1991): 204–9.

Kant, Immanuel. *Basic Writing of Kant.* Edited by Allen W. Wood. Translated by Carl F. Friedrich. New York: Modern Library, 2001.

Kelly, Catriona. "History and Post-modernism, II." *Past and Present: A Journal of Historical Studies* 133 (1991): 209–13.

Lamprecht, Karl. *Alternative zu Ranke: Schriften zur Geschichtstheorie.* Leipzig: P. Reclam, 1988.

———. *What Is History?: Five Lectures on the Modern Science of History.* Translated by E. A. Andrews. New York: Macmillan, 1905.

León, Luis D. *La Llorona's Children: Religion, Life, and Death in the U.S.-Mexican Borderlands.* Berkeley: University of California Press, 2004.

Lewis, Reina, and Sara Mills, eds. *Feminist Postcolonial Theory: A Reader.* New York: Routledge, 2003.

Loomba, Ania. *Colonialism/Postcolonialism.* London: Routledge, 1998.

López, Alfred J. *Posts and Pasts: A Theory of Postcolonialism.* Albany: State University of New York Press, 2001.

Lüdtke, Alf, ed. *The History of Everyday Life: Reconstructing Historical Experiences and Ways of Life.* Translated by William Templer. Princeton, N.J.: Princeton University Press, 1995.

Lyotard, Jean-François. *The Postmodern Condition.* Translated by Geoff Bennington and Brian Massumi. Minneapolis: University of Minnesota Press, 1984.

Machado, Daisy L. "A Borderlands Perspective," in *Hidden Stories: Unveiling the History of the Latino Church,* ed. Daniel R. Rodríguez-Díaz and David Cortés-Fuentes. Decatur, Ga.: Asociación para la Educación Teológica Hispana, 1994.

———. *Of Borders and Margins: Hispanic Disciples in Texas, 1888–1945.* New York: Oxford University Press, 2003.

———. "Latino Church History: A Haunting Memory." *Perspectivas: Occasional Papers* 1, no. 1 (1998): 22–34.

Maldonado, David Jr., ed. *Protestantes/Protestants: Hispanic Christianity within Mainline Traditions.* Nashville: Abingdon, 1999.

Marcos, Subcomandante. *Los del Color de la Tierra: Textos Insurgentes.* Nafarroa, Spain: Txalaparta, 2001.

Martín Alcoff, Linda, and Eduardo Mendieta, eds. *Thinking from the Underside of History: Enrique Dussel's Philosophy of Liberation.* Lanham, Md.: Rowman & Littlefield, 2000.

Martínez, Juan Francisco. "Origins and Development of Protestantism among Latinos in the Southwestern United States, 1836–1900." Ph.D. dissertation, Fuller Theological Seminary, 1996.

———. *Sea la Luz: The Making of Mexican Protestantism in the American Southwest, 1829–1900.* Denton: University of North Texas Press, 2006.

Martínez Guerra, Juan F., and Luis Scott, eds. *Iglesias Peregrinas en Busca de Identidad: Cuadros del Protestantismo Latino en los Estados Unidos.* Buenos Aires: Ediciones Kairós, 2004.

———. *Los Evangélicos: Portraits of Latino Protestantism in the United States.* Eugene, Ore.: Wipf & Stock, 2009.

Martínez-Vázquez, Hjamil A. *Latina/o y Musulmán: The Construction of Latina/o Identity among Latina/o Muslims in the United States.* Eugene, Ore.: Pickwick, 2010.

———. "The Postcolonizing Project: Constructing a Decolonial Imaginary from the Borderlands." *Journal of World Christianity* 1, no. 2 (2009): 1–28.

Marty, Martin E. *Pilgrims in Their Own Land: 500 Years of Religion in America.* Boston: Little, Brown, 1984.

———. *Religion and Republic: The American Circumstance.* Boston: Beacon, 1987.

———. *Righteous Empire: The Protestant Experience in America.* New York: Dial, 1970.

———. *The Writing of American Religious History.* Munich: K. G. Saur, 1992.

Matovina, Timothy M. *Guadalupe and Her Faithful: Latino Catholics in San Antonio, from Colonial Origins to the Present.* Baltimore: Johns Hopkins University Press, 2005.

———. *Tejano Religion and Ethnicity: San Antonio, 1821–1860.* Austin: University of Texas Press, 1995.

Matovina, Timothy, and Gerald E. Poyo, eds. *¡Presente!: U.S. Latino Catholics from Colonial Origins to the Present.* Maryknoll, N.Y.: Orbis, 2000.

McCann, Carole R., and Seung-Kyung Kim, eds. *Feminist Theory Reader: Local and Global Perspectives.* New York: Routledge, 2003.

McGuire, Meredith B. *Lived Religion: Faith and Practice in Everyday Life.* New York: Oxford University Press, 2008.

McKinzie, Steve. "Saints and Revisionists: Refashioning the American Religious Narrative." *Cross Currents* 48, no. 1 (1998): 103–4.

McLeod, John. *Beginning Postcolonialism.* Manchester, UK: Manchester University Press, 2000.

Mead, Sidney E. *The Lively Experiment: The Shaping of Christianity in America.* New York: Harper & Row, 1963.

Medina, Lara. *Las Hermanas: Chicana/Latina Religious-Political Activism in the U.S. Catholic Church.* Philadelphia: Temple University Press, 2004.

Memmi, Albert. *The Colonizer and the Colonized.* Boston: Beacon, 1965.

Merk, Frederick. *Manifest Destiny and Mission in American History: A Reinterpretation.* Westport, Conn.: Greenwood Press, 1963.

Michaelsen, Scott, and David E. Johnson, eds. *Border Theory: The Limits of Cultural Politics.* Minneapolis: University of Minnesota Press, 1997.

Mignolo, Walter D. *The Darker Side of the Renaissance: Literacy, Territoriality, & Colonization.* Ann Arbor: University of Michigan Press, 1995.

———. *Local Histories/Global Designs: Coloniality, Subaltern Knowledges, and Border Thinking.* Princeton, N.J.: Princeton University Press, 2000.

Miller, Page Putnam, ed. *Reclaiming the Past: Landmarks of Women's History.* Bloomington: Indiana University Press, 1992.

Mohanty, Chandra Talpade. *Feminism Without Borders: Decolonizing Theory, Practicing Solidarity.* Durham, N.C.: Duke University Press, 2003.

Mongia, Padmini, ed. *Contemporary Postcolonial Theory: A Reader.* London: Arnold, 1996.

Montejano, David. *Anglos and Mexicans in the Making of Texas, 1836–1986.* Austin: University of Texas Press, 1987.

Moore, R. Laurence. *Religious Outsiders and the Making of Americans.* New York: Oxford University Press, 1986.

Moraña, Mabel, Enrique Dussel, and Carlos A. Jáuregui, eds. *Coloniality at Large: Latin America and the Postcolonial Debate.* Durham, N.C.: Duke University Press, 2008.

Munslow, Alan. *Deconstructing History.* London: Routledge, 1997.

———. *The Routledge Companion to Historical Studies.* London: Routledge, 2000.

Náñez, Alfredo. *History of the Río Grande Conference of the United Methodist Church.* Dallas: Bridwell Library, Southern Methodist University, 1980.

Niebuhr, H. Richard. *The Kingdom of God in America.* Hanover, N.H.: Wesleyan University Press, 1988. Originally published by Willett, Clark, 1937.

———. *The Social Sources of Denominationalism.* Cleveland: World Publishing, 1929.

Nietzsche, Friedrich. *On the Advantage and Disadvantage of History for Life.* Translated by Peter Preuss. Indianapolis: Hackett, 1980.

Noll, Mark A. *A History of Christianity in the United States and Canada.* Grand Rapids: Eerdmans, 1992.

Olmstead, Clifton E. *History of Religion in the United States.* Englewood Cliffs, N.J.: Prentice Hall, 1960.

Orsi, Robert A. *The Madonna of 115th Street: Faith and Community in Italian Harlem, 1880–1950.* New Haven, Conn.: Yale University Press, 2002.

Padilla, Alvin, Roberto Goizueta, and Eldin Villafañe, eds. *Hispanic Christian Thought at the Dawn of the 21st Century: Apuntes in Honor of Justo L. González.* Nashville: Abingdon, 2005.

Penner, Todd, and Caroline Vander Stichele, eds. *Her Master's Tools? Feminist and Post-colonial Engagements of Historical-Critical Discourse.* SBL Global Perspectives on the Bible 9. Atlanta: Society of Biblical Literature, 2005.

Pérez, Emma. *The Decolonial Imaginary: Writing Chicanas into History.* Bloomington: Indiana University Press, 1999.

Pietersen, Jan Nederveen, and B. Parekh. *The Decolonization of Imagination: Culture, Knowledge and Power.* London: Zed Books, 1995.

Poster, Mark. *Cultural History and Postmodernity: Disciplinary Readings and Challenges.* New York: Columbia University Press, 1997.

Poyo, Gerald E. *Cuban Catholics in the United States, 1960–1980: Exile and Integration.* Notre Dame: University of Notre Dame Press, 2007.

Poyo, Gerald E., and Gilberto M. Hinojosa. "Spanish Texas and Borderlands Historiography in Transition: Implications for United States History." *Journal of American History* 75, no. 2 (1988): 393–416.

Pozzetta, George E., ed. *The Immigrant Religious Experience.* New York: Garland, 1991.

Prakash, Gyan, ed. *After Colonialism: Imperial Histories and the Postcolonial Displacements.* Princeton, N.J.: Princeton University Press, 1995.

Pulido, Alberto. *The Sacred World of the Penitentes.* Washington, D.C.: Smithsonian Institution Press, 2000.

Quayson, Ato. *Postcolonialism: Theory, Practice or Process?* Cambridge, UK: Polity, 2000.

Rajan, Gita, and R. Mahanram. *Postcolonial Discourse and Changing Cultural Contexts: Theory and Criticism*. London: Greenwood Press, 1995.

Recinos, Harold J. "Race Matters in More than Black and White." *Perspectivas: Occasional Papers* 1, no. 2 (1999): 1–16.

Ricoeur, Paul. *Time and Narrative*. Vol. 1. Translated by Kathleen McLaughlin and David Pellauer. Chicago: University of Chicago Press, 1984.

Rodríguez-Díaz, Daniel R., and David Cortés-Fuentes, eds. *Hidden Stories: Unveiling the History of the Latino Church*. Decatur, Ga.: Asociación para la Educación Teológica Hispana, 1994.

Rosaldo, Renato. *Culture & Truth: The Remaking of Social Analysis*. Boston: Beacon, 1989.

Rowe, Henry. *The History of Religion in the United States*. New York: Macmillan, 1924.

Ruether, Rosemary Radford, and Rosemary Skinner, eds. *Women and Religion in America: A Documentary History*. 3 vols. New York: Harper & Row, 1981–1985.

Ruha, Ganajit, and Gayatri C. Spivak. *Selected Subaltern Studies*. New York: Oxford University Press, 1988.

Said, Edward W. *Culture and Imperialism*. New York: Vintage, 1993.

———. *Orientalism*. New York: Vintage, 1978.

Saldívar, José David. *Border Matters: Remapping American Cultural Studies*. Berkeley: University of California Press, 1997.

Saldívar-Hull, Sonia. *Feminism on the Border: Chicana Gender Politics and Literature*. Berkeley: University of California Press, 2000.

Sánchez Walsh, Arlene M. *Latino Pentecostal Identity: Evangelical Faith, Self, and Society*. New York: Columbia University Press, 2003.

Sandoval, Chela. *Methodology of the Oppressed*. Minneapolis: University of Minnesota Press, 2000.

Sandoval, Moises, ed. *Fronteras: A History of the Latin American Church in the USA since 1513*. San Antonio, Tex.: Mexican American Cultural Center, 1983.

———. *On the Move: A History of the Hispanic Church in the United States*. Maryknoll, N.Y.: Orbis, 1990.

San Juan, Epifanio Jr. *Beyond Postcolonial Theory*. New York: St. Martin's, 1998.

Santiago-Valles, Kelvin A. *"Subject People" and Colonial Discourses: Economic Transformation and Social Disorder in Puerto Rico, 1898–1947*. Albany: State University of New York Press, 1994.

Schwarz, Henry, and Sangeeta Ray, eds. *A Companion to Postcolonial Studies*. Malden, Mass.: Blackwell, 2000.

Scott, Joan Wallach. *Gender and the Politics of History*. New York: Columbia University Press, 1999.

Singh, Amritji, and Peter Schmidt, eds. *Postcolonial Theory and the United States: Race, Ethnicity, and Literature*. Jackson: University of Mississippi Press, 2000.

Smith, H. Shelton, Robert T. Handy, and Lefferts A. Loetscher. *American Christianity: An Historical Interpretation with Representative Documents*. 2 vols. New York: Charles Scribner's Sons, 1960–1963.

Soja, Edward W. *Thirdspace: Journeys to Los Angeles and Other Real-and-Imagined Places*. Malden, Mass.: Blackwell, 1996.

Spiegel, Gabrielle. "History, Historicism, and the Social Logic of the Text in the Middle Ages." *Speculum* 65, no. 1 (1990): 59–86.

Stevens-Arroyo, Anthony, and Gilbert R. Cadena, eds. *Old Masks, New Faces: Religion and Latino Identities*. New York: Bildner Center for Western Hemisphere Studies, 1995.

Stone, Lawrence. "History and Post-modernism." *Past and Present: A Journal of Historical Studies* 131 (1991): 217–18.

———. "History and Post-modernism, III." *Past and Present: A Journal of Historical Studies* 135 (1992): 189–94.

Stout, Harry S. "Ethnicity: The Vital Center of Religion in America." *Ethnicity* 2 (1975): 204–24.

Stout, Harry S., and D. G. Hart, eds. *New Directions in American Religious History*. New York: Oxford University Press, 1997.

Sweet, William Warren. *The American Churches: An Interpretation*. New York: Abingdon-Cokesbury, 1947.

———. *The Story of Religions in America*. New York: Harper & Brothers, 1930.

Taylor, George Rogers, ed. *The Turner Thesis: Concerning the Role of Frontier in American History*. Lexington, Mass.: D. C. Heath, 1956.

Treviño, Roberto R. *The Church in the Barrio: Mexican American Ethno-Catholicism in Houston*. Chapel Hill: University of North Carolina Press, 2006.

Trouillot, Michel-Rolph. *Silencing the Past: Power and the Production of History*. Boston: Beacon, 1995.

Turner, Frederick Jackson. *The Frontier in American History*. New York: Holt, Rinehart & Winston, 1962.

Tweed, Thomas A. *Crossing and Dwelling: A Theory of Religion*. Cambridge, Mass.: Harvard University Press, 2008.

———. *Our Lady of the Exile: Diasporic Religion at a Cuban Catholic Shrine in Miami*. New York: Oxford University Press, 1997.

———, ed. *Retelling U.S. Religious History*. Berkeley: University of California Press, 1997.

Vandermeer, Philip R., and Robert P. Swierenga, eds. *Belief & Behavior: Essays in the New Religious History*. New Brunswick, N.J.: Rutgers University Press, 1991.

Vasquez, Manuel A. *More Than a Belief: A Materialist Theory of Religion*. New York: Oxford University Press, 2010.

Vélez-Ibáñez, Carlos G. *Border Visions: Mexican Cultures of the Southwest United States*. Tucson: University of Arizona Press, 1996.

Villafañe, Eldin. *The Liberating Spirit: Toward an Hispanic American Pentecostal Social Ethic*. Grand Rapids: Eerdmans, 1993.

von Ranke, Leopold. *The Secret of World History: Selected Writings on the Art and Science of History.* Edited and translated by Roger Wines. New York: Fordham University Press, 1981.

———. *The Theory and the Practice of History.* Edited by Georg G. Iggers and Konrad von Moltke. Translated by Wilma A. Iggers and Konrad von Moltke. Indianapolis: Bobbs-Merrill, 1973.

Walker, Randi Jones. *Protestantism in the Sangre de Cristos, 1850–1920.* Albuquerque: University of New Mexico Press, 1991.

Weber, David J, ed. *The Idea of Spanish Borderlands.* New York: Garland, 1991.

———. "John Francis Bannon and the Historiography of the Spanish Borderlands: Retrospect and Prospect." *Journal of the Southwest* 29, no. 4 (1987): 331–63.

———. *Myth and the History of the Hispanic Southwest.* Albuquerque: University of New Mexico Press, 1988.

———. *The Spanish Frontier in North America.* New Haven, Conn.: Yale University Press, 1992.

Weinberg, Albert K. *Manifest Destiny: A Study of Nationalist Expansionism in American History.* Chicago: Quadrangle, 1935.

White, Hayden. *The Content of the Form: Narrative Discourse and Historical Representation.* Baltimore: Johns Hopkins University Press, 1987.

———. *Metahistory: The Historical Imagination in Nineteenth-Century Europe.* Baltimore: Johns Hopkins University Press, 1973.

———. *Tropics of Discourse: Essays in Cultural Criticism.* Baltimore: Johns Hopkins University Press, 1978.

Williams, Patrick, and Laura Chrisman, eds. *Colonial Discourse and Post-colonial Theory: A Reader.* New York: Columbia University Press, 1994.

Williams, Peter W. *America's Religions: Traditions and Cultures.* New York: Macmillan, 1990.

———, ed. *Perspectives on American Religion and Culture.* Malden, Mass.: Blackwell, 1999.

Winner, Lauren F. "Retold, Redirected, Rethunk: Form and Content in the Study of American Religion." *Books and Culture: A Christian Review* 4, no. 3 (1998): 20–21.

Worcester, Donald E. "The Significance of the Spanish Borderlands to the United States." *Western Historical Quarterly* 7, no. 1 (1976): 5–18.

Wuthnow, Robert. *The Restructuring of American Religion: Society and Faith since World War II.* Princeton, N.J.: Princeton University Press, 1988.

Young, Robert. *White Mythologies: Writing History and the West.* London: Routledge, 1990.

INDEX